Document-Based Assessment
for U.S. History

MIDDLE SCHOOL

Kenneth Hilton

The classroom teacher may reproduce materials in this book for classroom use only.
The reproduction of any part for an entire school or school system is strictly prohibited.
No part of this publication may be transmitted, stored, or recorded in any form
without written permission from the publisher.

1   2   3   4   5   6   7   8   9   10
ISBN 0-8251-5904-0
Copyright © 2006
J. Weston Walch, Publisher
P.O. Box 658 • Portland, Maine 04104-0658
walch.com
Printed in the United States of America

CONTENTS

TO THE STUDENT

It sometimes seems as if history is presented in textbooks as a logical story line. It almost appears preplanned, proceeding step-by-step toward our time. This is a false perception. But from our vantage point in the present, it can seem this way. Unlike those who actually lived through the events of the past, we know how it all turned out. Knowing how the story ends distorts our view of the past and of those who lived in it. It creates a feeling that history was beyond human control, that people were powerless to shape events and outcomes. Nothing could be more wrong.

People shaped our past, just as other people will shape our future. Admittedly some events, such as hurricanes or earthquakes, are beyond human control. Also, no doubt, luck plays a role. But much is within our control. Our lives and the events of our times—past, present, and future—are largely results of decisions we make or actions we take, either alone or together with others. Let's test this by looking back in our nation's history to some of those events and to some of those decisions.

Most of us are descendents of those who asked, "Should I move to America?" Those early immigrants had to decide, "Where should I live? How shall I make my living?" Americans in the 1770s asked themselves, "Should America throw off English control?" Individual men and women wondered, "Should I remain loyal to England, or should I join this revolt?" Fifteen years later Americans asked, "Is this Constitution a good framework for our new government? Should we approve it?" A later generation of Americans asked, "Is slavery an evil practice that should be ended?"

Later generations of Americans were faced with new challenges and questions. In 1914, they asked themselves, "Should we enter the Great War in Europe or stay out?" Four times in the 1930s and 1940s Americans asked themselves, "Should we elect Franklin Roosevelt to be our president?" In our time we've asked ourselves, "Was the United States right to invade Iraq?" Each generation, facing the events and challenges of the past, had to make decisions. Your generation will do the same. It's these decisions and choices that drive history.

Your lives today were shaped by actions taken and decisions made by your parents and grandparents. Perhaps they, like earlier people, decided to move to America from other countries. Just like others before them, they may have had to struggle with difficult times and tough choices. At various times over the near past they faced major questions: "Should we change our tax system?" "How should we deal with economic hard times?" "How can we, as a nation, afford the huge costs of medical care?" "Do antipollution laws hurt the U.S. economy and cost Americans jobs?" "Who has the most effective plans for America's future, the Democrats or the Republicans?" Americans of your parents' and grandparents' generations addressed (or ignored) these and many other issues of the past several decades. In doing so, they have created your world.

You will shape the future history of our country. Your story will be part of that history. Just like those who came before you, you will be faced with challenges and choices. The choices you make will shape your future. Some of you will choose to study hard, be disciplined and tough and determined, do well in school, go on to college and succeed in life. Others will choose other futures. Some will choose to work together with people to achieve common goals. Perhaps they will strive to create a new town park or to provide after-school activities for school-age children. Perhaps they will work to support and elect a future mayor, governor, or president. Others will ignore society and its needs. They will choose not to vote or take part in the affairs and debates of their communities and country. Some of you will be active, make decisions, and make history. Others, who choose to be passive, will simply watch history happen.

Too often, students are passive as they study history. They see history as a meaningless collection of dates and names to be memorized for a test and then forgotten. They think of history as "settled," as the "officially approved" story, accepted by all. They overlook the controversies, the debates, the violence, and the human drama that mark history. They fail to see themselves in this story. They are unable to find their story, their purpose, their hopes and dreams in history. Don't be one of those passive students of history. Instead, be an active participant. See history not as a finished story but as an unfolding one. Be an active student of history, and be an active participant in the present and the future. Help to shape the story of your country.

This book invites you to take part in our country's past and in the decisions that shaped that past. It asks you to take sides in history's debates and controversies. It presents you with some of the same information that past Americans used as they struggled with major questions and issues. It asks you to join in those debates and decisions. This book asks YOU about major events in our nation's past. What would you have done? What is the meaning of those actions? Were decisions that were made in the past good or bad for the United States? How are we—even today—affected by those decisions? How will present and future decisions shape the history that your children will study when they are your age?

Some people stand passively on the sidelines of history. Others choose to play. We hope you will be among the active players of our nation's future history.

What Is a Document-Based Question?

This book contains 20 document-based questions, or DBQs. Each is an essay question on a major topic or issue in U.S. history. Many of these DBQs are open-ended, posing questions that invite debate and will lead different students to take different positions. Following each document-based question are a number of related documents. Most are primary sources, offering "eyewitness" reports from people who lived during that time and who took part in the events being examined. These documents include such things as excerpts from diaries, letters, speeches, magazine or newspaper articles, testimony, and reports. Others are maps, pictures, graphs, and charts.

Many of these documents disagree, presenting opposing viewpoints. Some seem more persuasive and believable than others. Some are clearly biased, presenting only one side of the story. Others seem more objective, more balanced, and more truthful. Some documents are difficult to understand. They'll require you to read between the lines, to understand more than is stated, to find their meaning. All documents present a viewpoint. But as we all know, even two eyewitnesses of the same event, can "see" very different things. Sorting out the "truth" is very difficult work. Sometimes it's impossible.

GETTING STARTED: GUIDELINES FOR TEACHERS

The document-based questions in this book can be used in various ways—as independent student assignments, as classroom exercises, as formal student assessments, as group projects, to prepare for classroom debates or seminars, or for direct instruction. Like other student assessments, they can serve a variety of purposes. Many invite debate, asking students to take sides and marshal evidence in support of their position. Others include no real debate. They simply ask students to use the documents and their outside knowledge to support a common thesis. All DBQs in this book are designed to be used after students have studied a topic. Students will then bring to these tasks necessary foundational knowledge and understanding of the question.

Each DBQ is organized to help students make sense of the task and to help them understand the meaning of documents. Each DBQ begins with a historical background section, an introduction that provides context and information useful to students. Likewise, each of the individual documents that follow is introduced with information that often helps students. Students must carefully read these introductions. All DBQs include short summary questions after each document. These are designed to help students analyze and interpret documents and to focus this analysis on the primary question. Obviously, students' abilities differ, and some students may arrive in your classroom with little or no experience with DBQs. Some will find writing DBQ essays to be easy tasks; most will struggle. You'll need to provide good teaching and encouragement.

At the back of this book you'll find a variety of grading guidelines designed to help teachers (and students) evaluate and grade DBQs. The Grading Key include a brief summary and discussion of each of the documents. Recognizing that good DBQ essays includes relevant information from sources beyond the documents that are included, a sampling of pertinent information that students should have from classroom, textbook, and other learning is also included for each DBQ. The Grading Key also includes actual student answers for DBQ 4 with teacher-assigned grades and comments. These essays were written by seventh graders in test-like, timed settings, following completion of the pertinent unit of study. You'll find the general grading rubric used by the teachers in scoring these essays on pages x–xi of this book.

Writing a DBQ essay is a rigorous and challenging academic task. It requires first, the ability to read, understand, and correctly analyze a document. This, in itself, is difficult work. But then, students are asked to do much more, to take what they've learned from all of these documents, synthesize all of this with what they already know about the topic, develop and state a thesis that directly answers the question, and write a forceful, coherent, and persuasive essay that marshals appropriate evidence and documentation to support the thesis.

If this is the first time that students have been exposed to DBQs, you'll need to go slowly, build skills sequentially, and scaffold tasks. Be sure to write some of the DBQs yourself, both to model the process and to better understand what you're asking students to do. Ask students to keep portfolios of their completed and graded DBQs so that they see how quickly they improve. Post excellent papers as models, and review them as a class so that all students begin to internalize the design and attributes of excellent answers. As you do with everything you teach, you'll build students' competence and confidence together, over time. Virtually all students can become proficient DBQ writers. Show them how.

Students will not be able to complete DBQs, start-to-finish, in one class period or one sitting, even if they've had some prior experience with them. Indeed, you can expect that few students will have had much, if any, experience with DBQs. The twenty DBQs included here will take your class through U.S. history from the first unit in your textbook right up to the present. They're designed, in general, to be used as group or whole-class work, with you facilitating. Typically, it's only after you've collectively read the Historical Background and reviewed the documents that you should expect students independently to write good DBQ essays. Go slowly early in the school year. You'll want to devote two or three class periods to many of these early DBQs. You may want to assign students to complete some DBQs in groups or pairs. As the year progresses and students do more DBQs, their proficiency (and their speed) will grow. By midyear most students will be ready to write the DBQ essays independently, in one sitting, but only after reviewing and discussing the content.

GETTING STARTED: GUIDELINES FOR STUDENTS

The twenty document-based questions (DBQs) in this book are designed to help you become better historians and better citizens. In each DBQ, you'll be examining actual evidence about important topics and questions in our nation's history. You'll weigh this evidence against what you already know about these topics. Then you'll reach conclusions that answer the questions. This is what actual historians do. It's also what we all, as thoughtful citizens, do. As citizens, we examine evidence and information about questions and issues that affect us, our families, the community, the state, the nation, or the world. We weigh all of this against what we already know about the questions or issues. We formulate our beliefs. Then we decide, take positions on issues, and try to convince others.

Writing essay answers to document-based questions will help you become better thinkers, problem solvers, and citizens. You'll learn to detect biases and determine the importance of various pieces of evidence. You'll learn to question and evaluate what you already know (or think you know). You'll learn to formulate logical and defendable conclusions, using evidence to support those conclusions. Finally, you'll learn to express yourself in clear, thoughtful, and persuasive written language. This won't be easy. But you can do it.

How to Begin

1. Begin by carefully and thoroughly reading the Historical Background. It will provide you with valuable information.

2. Now, carefully read the DBQ question. Be sure you know what it's asking.

3. Ask yourself: "How would I answer this question if I had no documents to examine?" You've already studied the topic, read about it in your textbook, and talked about it in class. You're not beginning the process from square one. You know a lot about it already. Don't discount this knowledge. As you read the documents, build on your understanding.

4. Before you begin to examine the documents, take a few minutes to jot down what you already know. What names, dates, events, and other things do you know about this topic and question?

5. Read the question again. Then read each document, asking yourself how it adds to your understanding of the question. Don't skip the introductory comments. They will help you understand the documents and their meanings. As you read the introductions and the documents, underline things of special importance. Scribble quick notes in the margins. Ask yourself: How does this document help to answer the question? What is its major point? Does it present an objective and believable position? How does it change or reinforce my beliefs about the topic and the question?

6. You'll see that the DBQs ask brief questions after each document. These questions focus on the main idea of the document. They are designed to help you find the document's meaning. Write brief, accurate answers to these questions. They will help you later when you write your essay answer.

7. Now that you've read all of a DBQ's documents, you're ready to formulate a thesis statement that directly answers the document-based question. Take a stand and

state a position—one that directly answers the question.

8. Briefly outline your essay so that you prove your thesis with supportive evidence and information both from the documents and from knowledge you already have.

9. Carefully write your essay. Cite evidence from the documents that supports and strengthens your thesis. Refer to these documents and other evidence in clear and fluid language. Don't say, for instance, "As Document 4 states . . . " Instead, say, "As President Bush said in his Inaugural Address . . . "

Name _____   Date _____

A SCORING RUBRIC FOR TEACHERS AND STUDENTS

It's good to remember that there are no right or wrong answers for most of the DBQs in this book. Quite different positions can earn top scores. The quality of answers is based primarily on the strength of the thesis and on how well the student uses documents and other evidence to support it. High scores go to answers that are well written and that present believable, persuasive, and supported positions.

The following scoring rubric identifies the criteria used in scoring DBQ essay answers. You might want to try to score some of your own answers, or answers written by classmates. Also, ask your teacher, whenever the class completes a DBQ, to duplicate one or two of the best answers from your class to share with all students. That way you can all examine and discuss the factors that make for strong answers.

Here are standards for DBQ essay scores from 5 down to 0. You will earn one of these scores if the DBQ answer shows . . .

5	A strong thesis. It directly answers the question. A thorough understanding of the topic and question. Accurate use of all documents, and weighing of their value and truthfulness. Evidence from beyond the documents that is used to support the answer. Excellent organization; forceful, well-written prose; and proper spelling, grammar, and mechanics.
4	A thesis that answers the question. An understanding of the topic and question. Accurate use of most documents. Also, recognition that some documents are more valuable than others. Some evidence from beyond the documents used to support the answer. Clear organization and good writing; only minor errors in spelling, grammar, and mechanics.
3	A weaker thesis that may not adequately answer the question. A general understanding of the topic and question. Accurate use of some documents, inaccurate use of others. Simplistic analysis and inadequate understanding of documents. Little understanding of the biases or differing value of documents. Little, if any, evidence from beyond the documents used to support the answer. Weaker organization and prose. Errors in spelling, grammar, and mechanics that detract from the essay's quality.
2	A weak thesis that fails to adequately answer or even address the question. Only some understanding of the topic and question. Inaccurate use of most documents. Or, documents simply paraphrased with little understanding of their importance to the question. No use of relevant information from beyond the documents to support the answer.

1	A confused and unfocused thesis that fails to address the question.
	Almost no understanding of the topic or question.
	Little, if any, understanding of the documents and their usefulness.
	Documents being simply paraphrased, misunderstood, or ignored.
	No use of valid or helpful information from beyond the documents.
	Disorganized and unfocused writing, littered with errors in standard English.
0	No thesis; no attempt to address the question.
	No understanding of the topic or question.
	No use or only misuse and misunderstanding of the documents.
	No information from any learning beyond simply the documents used.
	A lack of organization and structure. Little attempt made. Blank paper.

DBQ 1: WHAT MOTIVATED EUROPEANS TO EXPLORE AMERICA?

Historical Background

Until almost 1500, only about 500 years ago, North and South America remained unknown to people living in Europe, Asia, or Africa. It seems likely that several centuries earlier a tiny number of fishermen from northern Europe had found their way to areas we now call Greenland and northeastern Canada. But this contact with America remained unknown to the rest of Europe. (In fact, it's probable that most of these fishermen, themselves, were unaware of what they had found or where they had been.) The rest of the world remained ignorant of America's existence.

Then, in the 1400s, a new interest in exploration arose among Europe's leaders. This new interest would soon result in Europeans' discovery of the Americas. That new interest grew, in large part, from a desire to buy products from Asia. Europe's contacts with the Middle East had grown during the Crusades. Also, Marco Polo, of Italy, had traveled to China and lived there for a number of years. His book about his travels became a best-seller in Europe. From the book, Europeans learned about the existence of spices, dyes, fruits, rich tapestries, and other desirable products in Asia. But the eastern overland route between Europe and Asia was too long and too costly to be practical. So explorers, with financial backing from the monarchs of Spain and Portugal, began to seek ocean routes. Sea travel would provide faster and cheaper trade routes to the rich products of India and China. Thus, in the late 1400s an Italian sea captain named Christopher Columbus approached Spain's king and queen. He proposed to reach Asia by sailing to the west. With the monarchs' support and funding, Columbus stumbled onto several Caribbean islands in the autumn of 1492. Europe had now "discovered" America.

■ **Directions:** The following question is based on the documents (1–3) that follow. Before reading these documents, be sure to

1. Carefully read and think about the document-based question that follows these directions.

2. Ask yourself: What do I already know about this question and its topic? What did I learn from reading the Historical Background section? If I had to answer the document-based question without reading any of the documents, what would I say?

3. Take a few minutes to jot down the major things you already know about this topic and question. What important names, dates, events, and major ideas do you already know?

4. Now read each document carefully. Ask yourself: How does this document help to answer the document-based question? Underline things of special importance and jot notes in the margins. If you're confused by or don't understand a document, go on to the next one. Later, if you have time, you can go back.

(continued)

DBQ 1: WHAT MOTIVATED EUROPEANS TO EXPLORE AMERICA? *CONTINUED*

5. Develop a thesis statement that directly answers the document-based question. You'll want to state this thesis early in your essay.

6. Briefly outline your entire essay. Make sure that what you say in it supports and proves your thesis statement. In your essay, plan how you'll use the information found in the documents and what you know already about this topic.

7. Carefully write your essay. As you include supportive information from documents, be sure to cite the sources of this information. This will add authority and credibility to what you're saying.

> **Question: What factors motivated Europe's discovery and exploration of the Americas in the 1400s and 1500s?**

PART A   The following documents will help you answer the document-based question. Read each document carefully. Answer the question or questions that follow each document.

Document 1

In the late 1400s, the pope, the leader of the Roman Catholic Church, was a very powerful and influential person. He was so powerful, in fact, that he could impose his authority on the governments of nations. Here is a document issued by Pope Alexander VI in 1493. This was soon after Columbus returned to Europe with news that he had happened upon a series of new lands (America). In this document, the pope's office identified one of the primary motives of exploration of these new lands. It expressed the motive in the form of a command to the Spanish government.

> We have . . . learned that you [have] discovered certain islands and mainlands . . . to the [purpose] that you might bring to the worship of our Redeemer [Jesus] and the profession of the Catholic faith to their residents and inhabitants . . . We command you [to] appoint . . . God-fearing . . . men, in order to instruct the . . . inhabitants and residents in the Catholic faith and train them in good morals.

What, according to the pope, was a major motive of early European exploration of America? _____

_____

(continued)

DBQ 1: WHAT MOTIVATED EUROPEANS TO EXPLORE AMERICA? *CONTINUED*

Document 2

This letter, written by Columbus to the Spanish government during his return voyage from America, revealed another motive for his exploration of the New World.

> In the earth are many mines of metals. . . . There is incalculable gold. . . . The men whom I am leaving there [in America] will discover a thousand other things of value.

What, according to this letter from Columbus, was a major motive of early European exploration of America? _____

_____

Document 3

It's good to remember that Europeans found the Americas by accident. Columbus wasn't hunting for a "new land." He was trying to get to China and India. The lands he encountered in 1492 were, he guessed, islands somewhere off of the coast of Asia. It would, he believed, only take a little more exploration to find mainland Asia. The following document comes from a book published in 1971 by Samuel Eliot Morison. He was a historian who taught at Harvard University from 1915 until 1955.

> As a literary wit remarked, America was discovered by accident, not wanted when found, and early explorations were directed at finding a way through or around it. Columbus's fourth voyage, starting in 1502, was a search for a [route] from the Caribbean to the Indian Ocean; Cabot died seeking a [route] through North America; and for the next eight decades all recorded voyages [to America] . . . were first and foremost, searches for the . . . Northwest Passage to fabulous Cathay [China].

Source: Samuel Eliot Morison, *The European Discovery of America: The Northern Voyages,* Oxford University Press, 1971.

What, according to this account, was a major motive of early European exploration of America? _____

_____

PART B   Essay: What factors motivated Europe's discovery and exploration of the Americas in the 1400s and 1500s?

DBQ 2: WHY AND HOW DID PEOPLE COME TO EARLY AMERICA?

Historical Background

Americans have always been on the move. More than most other people, we seem to have a restless urge to relocate. In fact, each year almost one in every five Americans moves from one home to another. Sometimes these moves are just across the street or around the block. But many Americans move hundreds or thousands of miles to different states or even to different countries. Close to 100 million Americans (one in every three) were born in a different state from the one they presently live in. Almost 25 million were born in other countries. Today, as in the past, relatively few Americans live their entire lives in the towns in which they were born.

People move for many reasons. Perhaps your family is one of those who have moved in recent years. If so, you might ask your mom or dad to explain why your family moved. Very often the reason is economic—a better job or better job opportunities. Sometimes it's to be near family or friends. Sometimes people move to escape where they were; sometimes they're drawn to someplace new. Sometimes people have no choice. They simply have to move.

Many of the people who first came to America during its early colonial days moved here for the same reasons that people might relocate today. Many of these were the same reasons why immigrants still come to America today from other countries. The abundance of cheap, productive farmland drew many farmers from Europe. In Europe, land was scarce and rents were very high. In America, labor was scarce, so wages were higher than in Europe. This attracted many European workers to the colonies. Some early colonists came here with unrealistic dreams that they would quickly become wealthy. Some early colonial immigrants came to America to flee wars. Others came to escape religious persecution and oppressive rulers. Many simply realized that their lives back home in Europe held little promise. They hoped that America might provide a chance for better lives for themselves and for their families. These hopes fueled their migration.

■ **Directions:** The following question is based on the documents (1–5) that follow. Before reading these documents, be sure to

1. Carefully read and think about the document-based question that follows these directions.

2. Ask yourself: What do I already know about this question and its topic? What did I learn from reading the Historical Background section? If I had to answer the document-based question without reading any of the documents, what would I say?

3. Take a few minutes to jot down the major things you already know about this topic and question. What important names, dates, events, and major ideas do you already know?

(continued)

DBQ 2: WHY AND HOW DID PEOPLE COME TO EARLY AMERICA? *CONTINUED*

4. Now read each document carefully. Ask yourself: How does this document help to answer the document-based question? Underline things of special importance and jot notes in the margins. If you're confused by or don't understand a document, go on to the next one. Later, if you have time, you can go back.

5. Develop a thesis statement that directly answers the document-based question. You'll want to state this thesis early in your essay.

6. Briefly outline your entire essay. Make sure that what you say in it supports and proves your thesis statement. In your essay, plan how you'll use the information found in the documents and what you know already about this topic.

7. Carefully write your essay. As you include supportive information from documents, be sure to cite the sources of this information. This will add authority and credibility to what you're saying.

Question: Why and how did people come to settle in colonial America?

PART A The following documents will help you answer the document-based question. Read each document carefully. Answer the question or questions that follow each document.

Document 1

It's good to remember that not all colonial Americans voluntarily chose to come to America. Here is a brief excerpt from the autobiography of an African man named Olaudah Equiano. He was kidnapped as a boy in the mid-1700s. He was then brought to America, where he was sold into slavery.

After being kidnapped near his home in a western African village, he was marched to the coast with others.

> The first object which [I saw] when I arrived on the coast was the sea, and a slave ship . . . riding at anchor and waiting for its cargo . . . I was soon put down under the decks. . . .

Equiano spent weeks onboard the slave ship, filled with fear and sick from hunger and illness. When they finally landed in America, he and the other captives were very frightened. They feared that they would be killed.

(continued)

DBQ 2: WHY AND HOW DID PEOPLE COME TO EARLY AMERICA? CONTINUED

> . . . at last the white people got some old slaves from the land to pacify us. They told us we were not to be eaten, but to work . . .

Source: Olaudah Equiano, *The Interesting Narrative of the Life of Olaudah Equiano, the African.* Originally published in 1791.

Why and how did Olaudah Equiano (and thousands of others like him) come to colonial America? _____

_____

_____

Document 2

Large numbers of white people came to colonial America as indentured servants. Most were young, unmarried men. Some women and families also came as indentured servants. They were bound by an indenture, or contract, to serve their masters for a certain number of years. Most served as farm laborers, living very much like black slaves. As indentured servants, they had few rights. Sometimes families were broken apart. Most indentured servants voluntarily chose to "sell" themselves to pay the cost of their transport to America. Some, however, were forced into their indentures. Many of these involuntary indentured servants were minor convicts. The British government sent them to America to save the cost of keeping them in jails.

Black slaves remained bound for their entire lives. But indentured servants were bound by their indenture for only a few years. Once they completed their terms of service, they became free. Their master or their colony gave them land and tools. Society encouraged them to become independent farmers and good citizens. Most did. In the mid-1700s, a German visitor named Gottlieb Mittelberger traveled in Pennsylvania and other American colonies. He later wrote about this visit. In the excerpt below, he described the nature of indentured servitude in colonial America.

> Every day [colonists] go on board the newly arrived vessel that has brought people from Europe and offers them for sale. Then they negotiate with them as to the length of the period for which they will go into service in order to pay off their passage. . . . When an agreement has been reached, adult persons . . . bind themselves to serve for three, four, five, or six years, according to their health and age. The very young . . . have to serve until they are 21 . . . Work is strenuous in this new land. . . . Many [of] advanced age must labor hard for their bread. . . .

Source: Gottlieb Mittelberger, *Journey to Pennsylvania.* Originally published in 1754.

(continued)

DBQ 2: WHY AND HOW DID PEOPLE COME TO EARLY AMERICA? *CONTINUED*

Why did many people come to early colonial America as indentured servants? _____

_____

_____

Document 3

Many of the immigrants to America in the 1600s and 1700s were peasants and tenant farmers from England, Scotland, and Northern Ireland. They were farm workers who lived on land rented from wealthy landowners. They had almost no hope of ever escaping poverty or of owning their own land. Imagine how ambitious tenant farm families reacted to the following announcement. The colonial government of Maryland wrote it in the mid-1600s. The statement circulated in London and other cities in England, Scotland, and Northern Ireland.

> Any married man that shall transport himself, his wife and children, shall have assigned to him . . . [and his heirs] forever . . . for himself 100 acres, and for his wife 100 acres and for every child . . . 50 acres . . .

Why did this written announcement encourage many British tenant farmers to come to the American colonies? _____

_____

_____

Most peasants had no money to pay the cost of their trip to America. How could they go if they had no money to pay for the transportation? _____

_____

_____

Document 4

The promise of cheap land and hopes for wealth were lures for most poor European immigrants to early colonial America. But many others came here seeking something else. Among them were the early settlers of New England. The following are excerpts from the personal accounts of William Bradford, the first governor of Plymouth Colony. Here he tells why the Pilgrims chose to come to America.

(continued)

DBQ 2: WHY AND HOW DID PEOPLE COME TO EARLY AMERICA? *CONTINUED*

> . . . at length the conclusion was to live as a distinct [group] by themselves [in America] and to [seek from the king] freedom of religion.

While still onboard their ship, before landing on the coast, Bradford and other leaders of the group wrote and signed an agreement. It came to be known as the Mayflower Compact. One part of it stated

> We . . . [have] undertaken, for the glory of God and advancement of the Christian faith . . . a voyage to plant the first colony in the northern part of Virginia. . . .

Source: William Bradford, *Of Plymouth Plantation*. Originally published in 1856.

Why did Bradford and many others come to Plymouth Colony and later to Massachusetts in the early and mid-1600s? _____

_____

_____

_____

Document 5

Many poor people in Europe during the 1600s suffered daily injustices and persecutions. Farm peasants had to pay very high rents to the wealthy landowners. These peasants often were forbidden to hunt or fish on the lands they lived on. Their sons were forced into the army to fight the king's wars. The powerful landowners controlled the local government and courts. They used this control to benefit themselves and to deny rights and fairness to poor people. It was difficult for owners of small businesses to borrow money. Even when they could, they often had to pay very high rates of interest. Poor people had little power, and little hope.

The following excerpts come from a book written by an English traveler in colonial Pennsylvania and New Jersey. Contrast what he says about these American colonies with the description of life in Europe in the paragraph above.

(continued)

8

DBQ 2: WHY AND HOW DID PEOPLE COME TO EARLY AMERICA? *CONTINUED*

> . . . poor people (both men and women) of all kinds can here get three times the wages for their labor they can in England. . . .
>
> . . . their land costs them . . . little or nothing in comparison [to the price of land in England] . . . of which they will get twice the [value] of corn for every bushel they plant [than] the farmers in England can from the richest land they have.
>
> . . . they pay no tithes [church taxes equal to one tenth of a person's income], and their taxes are [minor]; the place is free for all [religions].
>
> . . . there . . . are schools of learning for youth . . .

Source: Gabriel Thomas, *Account of the Province and Country of Pennsylvania.*
Originally published in 1698.

How does this document help to explain why settlers from England and other areas of Europe chose to settle in colonial America? _____

_____

_____

_____

PART B   Essay: Why and how did people come to settle in colonial America?

DBQ 3: WHAT CAUSED THE AMERICAN REVOLUTION?

Historical Background

Too often, the seeds of future wars grow from the results of earlier wars. This certainly was true of the American Revolution.

The earlier conflict was the French and Indian War, which ended in 1763. Britain and its American colonies defeated the French and their Indian allies. This war was the last of a long series of colonial-era wars dating back to 1689. Britain and France fought these conflicts for control of Europe and of their colonies throughout the world. The French and Indian War (1754–1763) was the last of these conflicts. More than the earlier wars, it was waged over the control of North America. People in all the British North American colonies rejoiced at the British victory. In 1763, American colonists were proud to be part of the British Empire.

Yet in 1775, America and Britain were at war. How could Americans, in the space of only twelve years, go from celebrating their membership in the British Empire to waging war against Britain?

■ **Directions:** The following question is based on the documents (1–5) that follow. Before reading these documents, be sure to

1. Carefully read and think about the document-based question that follows these directions.

2. Ask yourself: What do I already know about this question and its topic? What did I learn from reading the Historical Background section? If I had to answer the document-based question without reading any of the documents, what would I say?

3. Take a few minutes to jot down the major things you already know about this topic and question. What important names, dates, events, and major ideas do you already know?

4. Now read each document carefully. Ask yourself: How does this document help to answer the document-based question? Underline things of special importance and jot notes in the margins. If you're confused by or don't understand a document, go on to the next one. Later, if you have time, you can go back.

5. Develop a thesis statement that directly answers the document-based question. You'll want to state this thesis early in your essay.

6. Briefly outline your entire essay. Make sure that what you say in it supports and proves your thesis statement. In your essay, plan how you'll use the information found in the documents and what you know already about this topic.

(continued)

DBQ 3: WHAT CAUSED THE AMERICAN REVOLUTION? *CONTINUED*

7. Carefully write your essay. As you include supportive information from documents, be sure to cite the sources of this information. This will add authority and credibility to what you're saying.

Question: What caused the American Revolution?

PART A   The following documents will help you answer the document-based question. Read each document carefully. Answer the question or questions that follow each document.

Document 1

Wars cost huge sums of money. After decades of war against France, Britain was deeply in debt in 1763. The government desperately needed money. British leaders expected the American colonies to help pay. After all, these wars had been waged, in large part, to protect the Americans from the French and their Indian allies. Raising taxes on the American colonists to help raise the needed funds seemed (to the British leaders) to be only fair and just. Surely, they thought, the Americans would agree.

One of the first taxes imposed by the British Parliament was commonly known as the Stamp Act. It required American colonists to pay fees on all kinds of printed documents. This included legal documents, licenses, newspapers, pamphlets, diplomas, and even decks of playing cards. John Adams was a young lawyer in Braintree, Massachusetts. He wrote a resolution protesting the Stamp Act. Braintree and many other towns in Massachusetts approved this resolution. The following excerpts come from that resolution.

> . . . the Stamp Act . . . a very burdensome and, in our opinion, unconstitutional tax is to be laid upon us all.
>
> . . . this tax [is] unconstitutional. We have always understood it be to a grand and fundamental principle . . . that no . . . man should be subject to any tax to which he has not given his own consent [by voting for those who pass such a tax].

Adams went on to protest the process by which the Stamp Act was supposed to be enforced. He described what would happen when someone was arrested and charged with violating the law:

(continued)

DBQ 3: WHAT CAUSED THE AMERICAN REVOLUTION? *CONTINUED*

> In the . . . courts one judge presides alone! No juries [are allowed]. This part of the act [violates our liberties and] is directly [opposed to our rights as Englishmen].

Source: Charles F. Adams, *Works of John Adams*, Vol. III, Boston, 1851.

Why were many American colonists outraged by the British Stamp Act? _____

_____

_____

Document 2

American colonists protested the Stamp Act and boycotted British imports. They threatened violence against anyone who tried to collect the taxes. In response, Parliament repealed the Stamp Act in early 1766. Most American colonists rejoiced at this action. They felt proud again to be English subjects. But Americans were alarmed at an official statement approved by Parliament at the time that it repealed the Stamp Act. This statement was called the Declaratory Act. It said that the British Parliament had the power to

> . . . make laws . . . to bind the colonies and people of America, subjects of the Crown of Great Britain, in all cases whatsoever.

What angered American colonists about the Declaratory Act? _____

_____

_____

Document 3

The next year, 1767, Parliament passed a new series of taxes called the Townshend Acts. American colonists now had to pay taxes on a number of popular British goods that they imported from England. These included items such as tea, paints, glass, ink, and dyes. Though these taxes were actually quite small, the outcry from many American leaders was huge. John Dickinson was a leading member of Pennsylvania's colonial government. He protested these taxes in a series of newspaper articles. The following excerpts come from those articles.

(continued)

DBQ 3: WHAT CAUSED THE AMERICAN REVOLUTION? *CONTINUED*

> There is another . . . act of Parliament which appears to me to be unconstitutional, and destructive to the liberty of these colonies. . . .

Most colonists accepted Parliament's authority to regulate trade. But Dickinson and many other colonial leaders were angry that the primary purpose of these taxes was to raise revenue for the British government. Three years earlier, John Adams had protested this in his attack on the Stamp Act. Dickinson agreed. Taxing the American colonists to raise money for the British government was unconstitutional. It was, as Dickinson said:

> A violation of our rights . . . to raise money upon us WITHOUT OUR CONSENT. . . .

Later in this article, Dickinson pleaded with his fellow American colonists:

> . . . my dear countrymen, ROUSE yourselves, and behold the ruin hanging over your heads. If you . . . admit that . . . Britain may [tax] us, for the purpose of levying money . . . without our consent . . . [then] we are . . . slaves. . . .

Source: John Dickinson, *Letters from a Farmer in Pennsylvania to the Inhabitants of the British Colonies.* Originally published in 1768.

Why, according to Dickinson, was it unconstitutional for Parliament to tax the colonists?

_____

_____

Reread the arguments used by Dickinson in Document 3 and Adams in Document 1. According to these arguments, who (or what) did have the constitutional authority to tax the colonists? _____

_____

Document 4

Opposition to British rule continued to grow among the American colonists. To protest against the Townshend Acts, colonists refused to buy imported (and taxed) goods from Britain. Meanwhile, British officials grew angrier at American acts of rebellion. The British became more determined to enforce their authority over the

(continued)

DBQ 3: WHAT CAUSED THE AMERICAN REVOLUTION? *CONTINUED*

colonists. In 1768, the British government sent several hundred British troops to Boston. This New England city was the center of the growing colonial unrest. The mission of the troops was to protect the tax collectors and other British officials. The people of Boston had seen British troops before. Soldiers had passed through the city on their way to fight, or coming back from fighting, the French and Indians. But these British troops stayed in Boston.

The colonists resented having British troops stationed in their city. Soon this resentment turned into anger and hatred. Occasional fights broke out between British soldiers and Americans—on the docks, in taverns, and on the streets. On the evening of March 5, 1770, a group of young men began pelting some British soldiers with snowballs and curses. A British officer and several soldiers came to the aid of their comrades. An angry crowd quickly assembled. More snowballs and curses, and now some cobblestones, flew at the soldiers. In the confusion, a scuffle broke out and the soldiers fired into the mob. They killed five Americans and wounded others.

The Sons of Liberty were a group of American colonists who favored independence from Britain. They labeled this unfortunate event the "Boston Massacre." One of their leaders, Paul Revere, engraved a picture of the "Boston Massacre." Hundreds of copies were printed. They were sent through all of the American colonies. These copies were reprinted in newspapers and posted on walls and trees. Thousands of people saw the image in the weeks that followed.

(continued)

14

DBQ 3: WHAT CAUSED THE AMERICAN REVOLUTION? *CONTINUED*

How does this picture portray the British soldiers and the Americans? Who seems to be at fault? _____

_____

_____

Does the picture portray the event of March 5, 1770, as it's described in the paragraph on the previous page? Explain. _____

_____

_____

Document 5

Tensions remained high during the months following the Boston Massacre. Growing numbers of colonists now favored independence from Britain. British officials became more convinced that they should counter colonists' actions with tough responses.

Still, cooler heads could have prevailed. Colonists were again drinking tea imported from Britain. Further violence and rebellion might have been avoided if calm could have been maintained.

But then, in December 1773, a new crisis developed. Several months earlier Parliament had granted to the British East India Company the sole right to sell tea to the American colonies. This made it possible for the company to lower the cost of tea for colonists. Some Americans were pleased that they could now buy tea at such low prices. But many others saw this as a British trick. They thought it was aimed at getting them to buy more tea and thus pay more of the hated tea tax. The Sons of Liberty warned British officials not to allow ships loaded with tea to come to America. But some did. On December 16, a group of rebellious colonists in Boston boarded three of these ships, broke into the cargo holds, and dumped 300 cases of tea overboard. When news of this "Boston Tea Party" reached London, members of Parliament were outraged. They passed what came to be known in America as the Intolerable Acts. These laws closed the port of Boston. They also banned town meetings throughout Massachusetts.

The other American colonies sympathized with Boston. They united to support the city. Colonial leaders called for the meeting of a Continental Congress. It met in the late summer of 1774 in Philadelphia. The Congress considered how to respond to Parliament's actions. The following are excerpts from resolutions passed by the First Continental Congress in October 1774.

(continued)

DBQ 3: WHAT CAUSED THE AMERICAN REVOLUTION? *CONTINUED*

> . . . the foundation of English liberty and of all free government is the right in the people to participate in their legislative council. . . .
>
> Resolved, That the following acts of Parliament are infringements and violations of the rights of the colonists; and that the repeal of them is . . . necessary in order to restore harmony. . . .
>
> . . . several acts . . . which impose [taxes] for the purpose of raising revenue. . .
>
> . . . acts . . . for stopping the port and blocking the harbor of Boston . . . keeping [British troops] in several . . . colonies in time of peace without the consent of the legislature[s]. . . .

The following year, in April 1775, war broke out. The American Revolution began.

According to the resolutions of the First Continental Congress, what brought the colonists to the brink of war with Britain in 1774? _____

_____

_____

 PART B   Essay: What caused the American Revolution?

DBQ 4: THE NEW CONSTITUTION: SHOULD IT BE APPROVED?

This DBQ asks you to be part of history. It asks you to experience an episode in our history from the viewpoints of the people who took part in it. As you complete this DBQ essay, imagine that you are living in 1788. Those who actually lived in 1788 and who took part in this episode in history didn't know how it would all turn out. Imagine that you don't know either. Use only information from the documents that follow and from your outside learning about this subject up to that year.

Historical Background (1788)

The years following the Revolutionary War were challenging ones. Yes, victory over the British had brought joy and pride. But people still struggled with many problems and faced some hard times. Among those problems were severe economic challenges. Wartime shortages of goods and the large-scale printing of almost worthless paper money caused inflation. This sent prices skyrocketing. Many families fell into poverty. Problems also arose in the relations that our young country had with other nations. The former colonies were no longer part of the powerful British Empire. Many other nations now felt free to ignore or even insult the new American country. People found it difficult to adjust to these and other new national problems.

Some of these problems grew from the shaky foundation and weak authority of our new national government. The Articles of Confederation had created what Americans of 1776 had wanted. The national government was weak, and the thirteen state governments were strong. Americans had just fought against a tyrannical king and central government in London. So the type of governmental balance created by the Articles seemed best. But now that Americans were free from British rule, they began to wonder if this balance was wrong. Without a stronger national government, America could command little respect from the world's nations. Even Great Britain ignored important clauses of the peace treaty that had ended the revolution. For instance, Britain refused to remove its troops from several forts in American territory.

Many Americans worried that the states might not stay united without stronger authority at the national level. Quarrels were occurring among the thirteen states. States were also displaying greater independence. Several states refused to pay their taxes to the national government. In 1786, a rebellion of poor Massachusetts farmers broke out. This event convinced many frightened Americans of the need for a stronger national government. Such a government would have the power to protect property and to maintain law and order. Some especially fearful Americans even began to talk hopefully of returning to a monarchy.

This was the situation in May 1787. That month, fifty-five representatives of twelve states met in Philadelphia to consider "revising" the Articles of Confederation. (Rhode Island refused to take part.) Four months later, their work was done. They had written a constitution that would scrap the Articles. It created in their place a national

(continued)

DBQ 4: THE NEW CONSTITUTION: SHOULD IT BE APPROVED? *CONTINUED*

government with certain powers over the states. It placed strong executive power into the hands of a national president. In September, the delegates approved the Constitution. They sent copies to the newspapers and to the state governments. They asked each state to hold a special convention. Delegates to these meetings would vote to approve or reject the proposed new Constitution.

Throughout America, a great debate began. Should the United States abandon its Articles of Confederation based on the strength of the states' powers? Or should America adopt this new Constitution and its stronger national government? This great debate led first to elections in each state for delegates to the state conventions for ratifying (approving) the Constitution. Then the debate focused on the decisions of these conventions.

You are now taking part in this great debate. Should the American people adopt the Constitution?

■ **Directions:** The following question is based on the documents (1–6) that follow. Before reading these documents, be sure to

1. Carefully read and think about the document-based question that follows these directions.

2. Ask yourself: What do I already know about this question and its topic? What did I learn from reading the Historical Background section? If I had to answer the document-based question without reading any of the documents, what would I say?

3. Take a few minutes to jot down the major things you already know about this topic and question. What important names, dates, events, and major ideas do you already know?

4. Now read each document carefully. Ask yourself: How does this document help to answer the document-based question? Underline things of special importance and jot notes in the margins. If you're confused by or don't understand a document, go on to the next one. Later, if you have time, you can go back.

5. Develop a thesis statement that directly answers the document-based question. You'll want to state this thesis early in your essay.

6. Briefly outline your entire essay. Make sure that what you say in it supports and proves your thesis statement. In your essay, plan how you'll use the information found in the documents and what you know already about this topic.

7. Carefully write your essay. As you include supportive information from documents, be sure to cite the sources of this information. This will add authority and credibility to what you're saying.

(continued)

DBQ 4: THE NEW CONSTITUTION: SHOULD IT BE APPROVED? *CONTINUED*

Question: Should Americans approve the new Constitution?

PART A The following documents will help you answer the document-based question. Read each document carefully. Answer the question or questions that follow each document.

Imagine that you're writing a newspaper editorial that either supports or opposes ratifying the new Constitution.

Document 1

As the debates over the new Constitution began in each state, it became obvious how sharply divided public opinion really was. Many Americans feared the creation of a new central government. They thought it would be out of touch with common people. Hadn't they just fought a war against a remote and out-of-touch central government in Britain? Hadn't this powerful central government violated the rights of the common people? Hadn't it threatened the rule of their locally elected governments? Why would they want to create a new, powerful central government? Wouldn't it be likely to act like a tyrant toward their state and local governments?

The following is an excerpt from a speech by Amos Singletary. He was elected as a delegate to the Massachusetts ratification convention. Many farmers and laborers supported his position.

> We [fought] with Great Britain . . . because they claimed a right to tax us and bind us in all cases . . . does not this Constitution do the same?
>
> These lawyers, and men of learning, and moneyed men, that talk so finely and gloss over matters so smoothly, to make us poor [uneducated] people swallow down the pill, expect to get into Congress themselves. They expect to be the managers of this Constitution, and get all the power and all the money into their own hands. And then they will swallow up all us little folks . . . this is what I'm afraid of. . . .

Source: Jonathan Elliot, ed., *The Debates in the Several State Conventions on the Adoption of the Federal Constitution*, Philadelphia, 1836.

(continued)

DBQ 4: THE NEW CONSTITUTION: SHOULD IT BE APPROVED? CONTINUED

Why did Singletary and many American farmers and laborers oppose the new federal Constitution? _____

_____

_____

Document 2

Many opponents of the new Constitution worried about the "supreme" powers that it placed in a central, national government. They feared this would be a threat to the rights of people. They also thought it would pose a danger to the power of the states. Many people also were concerned that the Constitution included few protections of individual freedoms and rights. (What we know today as the Bill of Rights is made up of the first ten amendments to the Constitution. They were not part of the original document. The Bill of Rights was added to the Constitution in 1791. This was three years after the debate over ratification was settled.)

One of the people who felt this way was a well-known Massachusetts woman named Mercy Otis Warren. She was a friend of John Adams and other political leaders of the time. She had been a major supporter of the revolution. Throughout her life, Mercy Otis Warren spoke out about the danger of strong government. It's no wonder that she opposed the U.S. Constitution. The following is an excerpt from an article she wrote that encouraged the Massachusetts convention to vote against its ratification.

> There is no security . . . for the rights of conscience or the liberty of the press.
>
> . . . it has been said that a standing army is necessary for the dignity and safety of America . . . [but] freedom revolts at the idea. A despot may quickly draw out his soldiers to suppress the [concerns] of the few.
>
> . . . the proposed constitution appears to [violate] the first principles that ought to govern humanity. [It seems to be] a step [toward] annihilation of the independence and sovereignty of the thirteen distinct states.

Source: Mercy Otis Warren, "Observations on the New Federal Constitution and on the Federal and State Conventions." Originally published in 1787.

Why did Warren oppose ratifying the new Constitution? _____

_____

_____

(continued)

DBQ 4: THE NEW CONSTITUTION: SHOULD IT BE APPROVED? *CONTINUED*

Do you think that her opinion about the Constitution would have been different if it had contained a Bill of Rights? Why? _____

_____

Document 3

Unlike Singletary and Warren (Documents 1 and 2), many Americans favored approval of the new Constitution. They wanted the new, more powerful national government that it proposed. Here is an excerpt from a pro-Constitution article. It was published in a Massachusetts newspaper during the debates of 1787.

> Let us look . . . [at] the distresses which prevail in every part of our country. Hear the complaints of our farmers. . . . Hear too the complaints of every class of public creditors. See the . . . bankruptcies. Look at the [sad] faces of our working people . . . without employment. . . . Listen to the insults that are offered to the American name. . . .
>
> View these things, fellow citizens, and then [try to] say that we do not require a new, a protecting, and efficient federal government. . . .

Source: *The Massachusetts Centinel*, October 20, 1787.

Why did the writer of this article favor ratification of the federal Constitution?

_____

_____

What do you suppose this writer had thought of Shays' Rebellion, which had occurred just the year before in 1786? Explain. _____

_____

Document 4

Joel Barlow was a schoolteacher and lawyer in Connecticut. During the American Revolution, he served as an army chaplain in the Continental Army. Later he became a well-known poet and statesman. On July 4, 1787, he gave a speech in Hartford, Connecticut. His listeners were a group of Revolutionary War veterans. (Remember, the Constitutional Convention was meeting at this time.) Here is a brief excerpt from that speech.

(continued)

DBQ 4: THE NEW CONSTITUTION: SHOULD IT BE APPROVED? *CONTINUED*

The Revolution is but half completed. Independence and government were the two objects [we fought] for, and but one is yet obtained. Without an efficient government, our independence will cease to be a blessing. [We should] unite in a permanent federal government.

Source: Joel Barlow. "An Oration Delivered by Mr. Joel Barlow at Hartford, Connecticut, to the Society of the Cincinnati, July 4, 1787."

Why did Barlow favor the new federal Constitution? _____

_____

What did he mean by saying, "The Revolution is but half completed"? _____

_____

Document 5

The delegates signed the Constitution in September of 1787. Among these people were some of the most well-known and respected men in America. They included Benjamin Franklin, George Washington, James Madison, and John Jay. Their support for the new Constitution was key. It helped to convince many Americans to favor the document's adoption. The following is an excerpt from a pamphlet Jay wrote in 1787, addressed to the people of his native New York State. The pamphlet encouraged them to support the ratification of the Constitution.

Reflect that the [Constitution] comes recommended to you by men and fellow citizens who . . . love their liberty and their country.

Jay went on to admit that the proposed Constitution might not be perfect. But he then made this request:

At least . . . give the proposed Constitution a fair trial, and to mend it as time, occasion, and experience may [require].

Source: John Jay, "An Address to the People of New York on the Subject of the Proposed Federal Constitution." Originally published in April 1788.

(continued)

DBQ 4: THE NEW CONSTITUTION: SHOULD IT BE APPROVED? *CONTINUED*

What arguments in favor of the new federal Constitution did Jay make in these statements? _____

_____

Document 6

Thomas Jefferson was the author of the Declaration of Independence. He played no role in the writing of the Constitution. At the time of the Constitutional Convention, Jefferson was in Paris. He was serving there as American minister to France. Soon after the Constitution was written, his friend James Madison sent Jefferson a copy. The following excerpts come from a letter that Jefferson sent Madison. He wrote it soon after he read the proposed Constitution. He supported parts of the document. But you will see that he strongly disliked at least one thing about the Constitution.

> There are other good things [about the Constitution, but] I will now add what I do not like. First, the omission of a bill of rights providing . . . for freedom of religion, freedom of the press, protection against standing armies . . . trials by jury. . . . Let me add that a bill of rights is what the people are entitled to. . . .

Source: Thomas Jefferson papers, letter, Jefferson to Madison, December 20, 1787.

What objection did Jefferson have to the new federal Constitution? _____

_____

_____

With which of Documents 1–5 would Jefferson most agree? _____

PART B   Essay: Should Americans approve the new Constitution?

For the essay, imagine that you're writing a newspaper editorial. It either supports or opposes ratifying the new Constitution.

DBQ 5: WHAT CHALLENGES DID GEORGE WASHINGTON FACE AS PRESIDENT?

This DBQ, unlike most others in this book, generates no real debate. It asks you to use the documents and your outside knowledge to support a common position.

Historical Background

George Washington never really ran for president. He loved his life at Mt. Vernon, his large plantation on the Potomac River in Virginia. In 1788, the Constitution was ratified and the new national government formed. Washington was fifty-six years old at this time, no longer young. He was tired of being away from home during the war years. He was very eager to return to Mt. Vernon. He hoped to spend his remaining years there surrounded by family and friends.

But the American people had other plans for Washington. No one was more popular and more respected. Most people expected that he would become our first president. When the electoral votes were counted, Washington had received all sixty-nine. Now he was president of the United States. He said that he felt "like a culprit who is going to . . . his execution" as he made his way to New York City. (This was the temporary capital of the new nation.) There, he would take his place at the head of the new government.

Eight years later, in 1797, Washington returned home at last to Mt. Vernon. He had completed his two terms as the first president of the new nation. Washington was exhausted, tired of political squabbles, and eager to escape the attacks of opposition newspapers. He wondered how future historians would see his presidency.

Today, over 200 years later, we see Washington's presidency as remarkably successful. As chief executive, Washington faced a variety of major challenges and crises. Yet he left our young government strong, sound, and secure.

■ **Directions:** The following question is based on the documents (1–6) that follow. Before reading these documents, be sure to

1. Carefully read and think about the document-based question that follows these directions.

2. Ask yourself: What do I already know about this question and its topic? What did I learn from reading the Historical Background section? If I had to answer the document-based question without reading any of the documents, what would I say?

3. Take a few minutes to jot down the major things you already know about this topic and question. What important names, dates, events, and major ideas do you already know?

(continued)

DBQ 5: WHAT CHALLENGES DID GEORGE WASHINGTON FACE AS PRESIDENT? *CONTINUED*

4. Now read each document carefully. Ask yourself: How does this document help to answer the document-based question? Underline things of special importance and jot notes in the margins. If you're confused by or don't understand a document, go on to the next one. Later, if you have time, you can go back.

5. Develop a thesis statement that directly answers the document-based question. You'll want to state this thesis early in your essay.

6. Briefly outline your entire essay. Make sure that what you say in it supports and proves your thesis statement. In your essay, plan how you'll use the information found in the documents and what you know already about this topic.

7. Carefully write your essay. As you include supportive information from documents, be sure to cite the sources of this information. This will add authority and credibility to what you're saying.

> **Question: What challenges did George Washington face during the eight years of his presidency?**

PART A   The following documents will help you answer the document-based question. Read each document carefully. Answer the question or questions that follow each document.

Document 1

Alexander Hamilton was a brilliant man. He had served General Washington during the Revolutionary War as a close and trusted aide. Now, as president, Washington turned to him again. He chose Hamilton to be our nation's first secretary of the treasury. (The treasury is the government department in charge of finances.) Hamilton's first goal was to pay off the country's huge debt. The states and the Continental Congress had run up these debts to cover the costs of the Revolutionary War.

In 1790, Secretary of the Treasury Alexander Hamilton sent a report to Congress. It outlined his financial plan for the national government. The report called for higher taxes and the creation of a national bank. It also recommended that the national government pay the Revolutionary War debts of the states.

Washington, himself, generally favored these proposals. But many other people did not. Some states had been frugal during the war. In the years after the war, they had heavily taxed their own citizens in order to pay off their debts. These states protested Hamilton's plan. Why, they asked, should their citizens now be taxed to pay the debts of the other, less-frugal states?

(continued)

DBQ 5: WHAT CHALLENGES DID GEORGE WASHINGTON FACE AS PRESIDENT? *CONTINUED*

The following is an excerpt from a resolution passed by the state legislature of Virginia in December of 1790.

> [We] can find no clause in the constitution authorizing Congress to assume the debts of the states. . . . The General Assembly of . . . Virginia . . . hope that [Congress] will . . . repeal [the proposal calling for] the assumption of the state debts.

Why, according to the resolution, did Virginia oppose Hamilton's plan to have the national government pay the debts of the states? _____

_____

The introductory paragraph before this document suggests another reason. What was it?

_____

_____

Document 2

Part of Hamilton's financial plan called for the establishment of a national bank. The Bank of the United States would collect all tax revenues. It would issue U.S. currency. It would make loans to support the growth of business and industry. Many Americans, especially farmers and debtors, opposed this proposal. They feared the great power of such an institution. Thomas Jefferson was President Washington's secretary of state. Washington asked Jefferson for his opinion of this proposal. The following excerpts are from Jefferson's memo back to the president. As you'll see, Jefferson firmly opposed the bank.

> The incorporation of a bank, and the powers assumed by this bill, have not, in my opinion, been delegated to the [national government].

Jefferson went on in this same document to point out some of the dangers and wrongs he saw in establishing the national bank.

> To give [it] the sole and exclusive right of banking under the national authority . . . is against the laws of monopoly . . . to [grant it] a power to make laws [superior] to the laws of states . . . [is wrong].

(continued)

DBQ 5: WHAT CHALLENGES DID GEORGE WASHINGTON FACE AS PRESIDENT? *CONTINUED*

What did Jefferson think about Hamilton's plan for a national bank? _____

_____

_____

Document 3

The financial plan was only one of many issues that pitted Jefferson against Hamilton. President Washington found himself struggling with public opinion split into two opposed groups. One supported Jefferson and his positions. The other supported Hamilton and his ideas. As the following excerpts show, the feud became bitter, mean, and nasty.

Here is an excerpt from a memo written by Jefferson in 1791. (A *monarchist* is a person who favors rule by a king or queen.)

> Hamilton [is] not only a monarchist, but . . . a monarchist bottomed on corruption. . . . [He is] so bewitched and perverted by the British example as to [believe] that corruption [is] essential to the government of a nation.

A few months later Hamilton wrote this about Jefferson. (By a *faction,* Hamilton means what we now call a political party.)

> Mr. Madison, cooperating with Mr. Jefferson, is at the head of a faction . . . hostile to me . . . and subversive of the principles of good government, and dangerous to the union, peace and happiness of the country. They have a womanish attachment to France, and a womanish resentment against Great Britain.

What did Jefferson and Hamilton think of each other? _____

_____

_____

Document 4

One of the issues dividing Jefferson and Hamilton, and their supporters, was the ongoing war in Europe. This war between Britain and France broke out in the early 1790s. In part, it was a response to the French Revolution, which had begun in 1789.

(continued)

DBQ 5: WHAT CHALLENGES DID GEORGE WASHINGTON FACE AS PRESIDENT? CONTINUED

President Washington knew that the U.S. military was weak. He also knew that the U.S. system of government was new and untried. He saw that to become involved actively in war with either Britain or France would have disastrous results for the United States. Washington was concerned that the American people were taking sides in this war. He was angry that Jefferson and Hamilton seemed to be encouraging this. Realizing the danger to our security, Washington issued the following statement on April 22, 1793. (*Impartial* means neutral.)

> Whereas it appears that a state of war exists between . . . Great Britain . . . on the one part and France on the other . . . the . . . interest of the United States require that [it] should with sincerity and good faith adopt and pursue a conduct friendly and impartial toward [both countries].

Source: James D. Richardson, *Messages and Papers of the Presidents*, Vol. I. Published in 1897.

Why did Washington issue this "Neutrality Proclamation"? _____

_____

_____

Document 5

Governments provide services to their citizens. They need money from taxes to pay for these services. Hamilton's financial plan found two tax sources for the new national government. Most revenue would come from tariffs. (*Tariffs* are taxes on imported goods.) The rest of the government's revenues would come from a tax on distilled liquor. The burden of this tax fell hardest on the farmers of the backcountry of western Virginia and Pennsylvania. They distilled much of their corn crop into whiskey for sale. The farmers' protests turned into outright refusal to pay the taxes. President Washington responded quickly and aggressively. Here are excerpts from a presidential proclamation announced in August 1794. (*Insurgents* are rebels.)

> Whereas, [groups have formed] to defeat the [enforcement] of the laws laying [taxes] upon spirits distilled within the United States . . . it is in my judgment necessary . . . for calling forth the militia in order to suppress the [revolt] . . . and to cause the laws to be duly [enforced].
>
> Therefore . . . I, George Washington, President of the United States, do hereby command all persons, being insurgents . . . to disperse and retire peaceably. . . .

(continued)

DBQ 5: WHAT CHALLENGES DID GEORGE WASHINGTON FACE AS PRESIDENT? *CONTINUED*

Why did President Washington feel that he had to act so quickly and firmly in this situation? _____

_____

How do you think Hamilton and Jefferson differed in their views of this Whiskey Rebellion? _____

_____

Document 6

George Washington served two terms as the first president of the United States. Near the end of his second term, he decided to write a farewell address to the American people. Alexander Hamilton helped prepare this statement. It was published in American newspapers in September 1796. In it, Washington shared his advice with Congress and with his fellow citizens. As you might expect, Washington's advice grew from his experiences as president. His words express his deepest concerns about the issues and challenges that he and the nation had faced during these years. Here are some key excerpts from the Farewell Address. (*Baneful* means destructive.)

> I . . . warn you in the most solemn manner against the baneful effects [of political parties].
>
> The great rule of conduct for us in regard to foreign nations is . . . to have with them as little political connection as possible. . . . [We must] steer clear of permanent alliances with any portion of the foreign world. . . .

What two major issues of his presidency was Washington referring to in these excerpts from his Farewell Address? _____

_____

Why do you suppose Washington was so concerned about these issues? _____

_____

_____

PART B

Essay: What challenges did George Washington face during the eight years of his presidency?

Document-Based Assessment for U.S. History

DBQ 6: WHY DO WE REMEMBER THOMAS JEFFERSON?

Historical Background

In all of our nation's history (into 2006) only forty-two men have served as president of the United States. Only a few of these presidents have their pictures on coins or bills. Only a few have had huge, majestic Washington, D.C., memorials built in their honor. Only a few are carved as giant granite symbols on the side of Mt. Rushmore. Only a few are ranked by our historians as truly great presidents. Only a few are revered in the public mind as symbols of our nation and its values. Thomas Jefferson is one of these very few who meet all of these descriptions. Today, almost 200 years after his presidency, Jefferson remains alive in the hearts and minds of Americans as a symbol of liberalism. What are the main elements of Jefferson's liberalism?

■ **Directions:** The following question is based on documents (1–5) that follow. Before reading these documents, be sure to

1. Carefully read and think about the document-based question that follows these directions.

2. Ask yourself: What do I already know about this question and its topic? What did I learn from reading the Historical Background section? If I had to answer the document-based question without reading any of the documents, what would I say?

3. Take a few minutes to jot down the major things you already know about this topic and question. What important names, dates, events, and major ideas do you already know?

4. Now read each document carefully. Ask yourself: How does this document help to answer the document-based question? Underline things of special importance and jot notes in the margins. If you're confused by or don't understand a document, go on to the next one. Later, if you have time, you can go back.

5. Develop a thesis statement that directly answers the document-based question. You'll want to state this thesis early in your essay.

6. Briefly outline your entire essay. Make sure that what you say in it supports and proves your thesis statement. In your essay, plan how you'll use the information found in the documents and what you know already about this topic.

7. Carefully write your essay. As you include supportive information from documents, be sure to cite the sources of this information. This will add authority and credibility to what you're saying.

Question: Thomas Jefferson, more than any other leader of our nation, is remembered as a symbol of liberalism. How would you define and describe the beliefs and values of Jeffersonian liberalism?

DBQ 6: WHY DO WE REMEMBER THOMAS JEFFERSON? *CONTINUED*

PART A The following documents will help you answer the document-based question. Read each document carefully. Answer the question or questions that follow each document.

Document 1

Lexington and Concord were villages just outside of Boston. The first fighting between the American colonists and British troops broke out at these villages in April of 1775. The Continental Congress voted in June of 1776 to "prepare a declaration" of independence. By that time, the war had been going on for fourteen months. All hope for a peaceful settlement and reunion with England was gone. America would fight for its independence.

The Continental Congress appointed a committee of five prominent members. These men included Thomas Jefferson, Benjamin Franklin, and John Adams. Their task was to act as a group and prepare a written statement. But soon the committee asked Jefferson to write the first draft. Jefferson was still a young man—he was only thirty-three years old. But he was widely known and admired for his clear, forceful, and eloquent writing. As Adams said to him, "You can write ten times better than I can."

In only two weeks, Jefferson completed the document. He made a few changes suggested by the committee members. Then the group submitted it to Congress on June 28. During debates on July 2 and 3, some additional revisions were made. But the document that was approved on July 4 was much the work of Thomas Jefferson. It was very much an expression of his beliefs. (We honor the Declaration on July 4 each year.) Here is a famous excerpt, one that Americans proudly recognize. (*Unalienable* means "undeniable." *Instituted* means "established." *Deriving* means "receiving.")

> We hold these truths to be self-evident, that all men are created equal, that they are endowed by their Creator with certain unalienable rights, that among these are Life, Liberty and the pursuit of Happiness. That to secure these rights, Governments are instituted among Men, deriving their . . . powers from the consent of the governed.

List the rights that Jefferson believed are held by all people. _____

_____

What, according to Jefferson, is the purpose of government? _____

_____

(continued)

DBQ 6: WHY DO WE REMEMBER THOMAS JEFFERSON? *CONTINUED*

Document 2

Thomas Jefferson served as our third president. He was first elected in 1800 and then reelected four years later. He gave his First Inaugural Address on March 4, 1801. It is known for outlining many of his most strongly held beliefs. Here are some excerpts from that speech. (*Deem* means "believe.")

> . . . you should understand what I deem the essential principles of our Government . . . the right of election by the people . . . freedom of religion; freedom of the press . . . trial by juries. . . . These principles . . . should be the creed of our political faith.

Source: P. L. Ford, ed; *The Writings of Thomas Jefferson.* Published in 1895.

According to Jefferson, what were the "essential principles" of American government?

_____

_____

_____

_____

Document 3

Perhaps more than any other president in all of our history, Jefferson is remembered as a champion of public education. He believed local taxes should support public education. He also believed that public education should be provided free of charge to the children of all families, rich and poor alike. Jefferson understood that education would improve the lives of individuals. But he also believed that education had the power to improve society as a whole. It could elevate the wisdom and good sense of the American public. He felt strongly that this "wisdom of the people" was needed to maintain a democratic society.

What follows are brief excerpts from several letters Jefferson wrote. They express his beliefs about education and its importance. (*Ameliorated* means "improved." *Effecting* means "accomplishing.")

(continued)

DBQ 6: WHY DO WE REMEMBER THOMAS JEFFERSON? *CONTINUED*

> If the condition of man is to be progressively ameliorated, as we fondly hope and believe, education is the chief instrument for effecting it.
>
> —from a letter written in 1818
>
> A system of general instruction, which shall reach every description of our citizens, from the richest to the poorest . . . [is my interest].
>
> —from a letter written in 1818
>
> If a nation expects to be ignorant and free . . . it expects what never was and never will be.
>
> —from a letter written in 1816
>
> No other sure foundation can be devised for the preservation of freedom and happiness [than education]. . . . Preach a crusade against ignorance; establish and improve the law for educating the common people.
>
> —from a letter written in 1786

Why, according to Jefferson, was a free public education so important to the United States? _____

_____

_____

Document 4

Jefferson believed in rule by the majority. He also believed in rights and protections for the minority. He felt that even unpopular opinions have the right to be voiced and to be heard. He knew the majority might want to suppress ideas they thought were wrong, or even repugnant. He said this would be wrong. Few other American leaders have been such strong defenders of the views and rights of others. Jefferson often urged tolerance for minority opinion all through his life. Perhaps his most eloquent expression is in his First Inaugural Address, given on March 4, 1801. (Note Document 2, on page 32.) The following excerpt comes from that speech.

(continued)

DBQ 6: WHY DO WE REMEMBER THOMAS JEFFERSON? *CONTINUED*

> All . . . will bear in mind this sacred principle, that though the will of the majority is in all cases to prevail, that will . . . must be reasonable; . . . the minority possess . . . equal rights, which equal law must protect, and to violate would be oppression.

Some people might argue that, in a democratic society, majority opinion should always rule. Would Jefferson agree? Explain. _____

_____

_____

Document 5

The United States is a nation of immigrants. All of us came here from other lands. Either we are immigrants ourselves, or we are the descendents of immigrants. Jefferson believed that America's borders should be open to future immigrants. He thought that they should have equal chances to thrive. The following brief excerpt comes from the "Proclamation Concerning Foreigners." Jefferson wrote this in 1781, while serving as governor of Virginia.

> It has been the wise policy of . . . states to extend the protection of their laws to all those who settle among them of whatsoever nation or religion they might be, and admit them to a participation of the benefits of civil and religious freedom.

Do you agree with Jefferson's position on immigration? Defend your position.

_____

_____

_____

 PART B Essay: Thomas Jefferson, more than any other leader of our nation, is remembered as a symbol of liberalism. How would you define and describe the beliefs and values of Jeffersonian liberalism?

DBQ 7: INDIAN REMOVAL: IS IT JUSTIFIED?

This DBQ asks you to be part of history. It asks you to experience an episode in our history from the viewpoints of the people who took part in it. As you complete this DBQ essay, imagine that you are living in the early spring of 1830. Those who actually lived at that time and who took part in this episode in history didn't know how it would all turn out. Imagine that you don't know either. Use only information from the documents and from your outside learning about this subject up to the early spring of 1830.

Historical Background

In January 1830, a bill entitled the Indian Removal Act was introduced into Congress. President Andrew Jackson strongly supported this law. It proposed that Congress open talks with the Indian tribes in the southeastern United States. The object was, first, to take their lands. Then the U.S. government would force these Indians to relocate west. They would move beyond the Mississippi River to the area we know today as Oklahoma.

At this time, approximately 100,000 Native Americans lived among five major tribes in the southeastern United States. The Cherokees lived in northern Georgia and western North Carolina. The Creeks lived largely in Alabama, just to the southwest of the Cherokees. The Chickasaw resided in northern Mississippi. The Choctaw lived in central Mississippi. The Seminoles resided in Florida. Many still lived as their ancestors had years earlier. Many others had gone far in accepting the values and lifestyles of U.S. white society. Many had become Christian. Some had become settled farmers. They adopted the farming methods of the whites. The Cherokees had even developed a written language. They had also adopted a written constitution, based on the U.S. Constitution.

The people of all of these tribes were living on their own lands. Years earlier, treaties with the United States government had granted these lands to them. But by the 1820s, nearby white settlement was growing. Farmers, prospectors, and others wanted the Indians' land. They put pressure on state governments to force the Indians off of their lands. In 1828, the Georgia state legislature passed a law that denied the right of the Cherokees to rule themselves. This law also divided Cherokee lands for future settlement by other people of Georgia. The Cherokees were alarmed. They began efforts to protect themselves and their treaty rights. They quickly filed suit in federal court. They asked the U.S. government to protect their treaty rights from being violated by Georgia.

This was the situation in the late winter and early spring of 1830 as Congress debated the Indian Removal Act. You, as a newspaper editor, must decide whether to support or oppose this proposed law. You must write and publish your editorial on this subject soon.

(continued)

DBQ 7: INDIAN REMOVAL: IS IT JUSTIFIED? *CONTINUED*

■ **Directions:** The following question is based on the documents (1–6) that follow. Before reading these documents, be sure to

1. Carefully read and think about the document-based question that follows these directions.

2. Ask yourself: What do I already know about this question and its topic? What did I learn from reading the Historical Background section? If I had to answer the document-based question without reading any of the documents, what would I say?

3. Take a few minutes to jot down the major things you already know about this topic and question. What important names, dates, events, and major ideas do you already know?

4. Now read each document carefully. Ask yourself: How does this document help to answer the document-based question? Underline things of special importance and jot notes in the margins. If you're confused by or don't understand a document, go on to the next one. Later, if you have time, you can go back.

5. Develop a thesis statement that directly answers the document-based question. You'll want to state this thesis early in your essay.

6. Briefly outline your entire essay. Make sure that what you say in it supports and proves your thesis statement. In your essay, plan how you'll use the information found in the documents and what you know already about this topic.

7. Carefully write your essay. As you include supportive information from documents, be sure to cite the sources of this information. This will add authority and credibility to what you're saying.

> **Question: It's April 1830, and Congress is debating the Indian Removal Act. Should this law be passed? Write a newspaper editorial that expresses your opinion.**

The following documents will help you answer the document-based question. Read each document carefully. Answer the question or questions that follow each document.

(continued)

DBQ 7: INDIAN REMOVAL: IS IT JUSTIFIED? *CONTINUED*

Document 1

The Indian Removal Act was proposed in Congress in January of 1830. Long before that, political leaders were concerned about the place of Indians within U.S. society. President James Monroe spoke of this concern to Congress. It was one of his last messages to Congress before retiring as president in 1825. Monroe spoke in general terms. He also talked about the situation of the Cherokees in Georgia. Here are excerpts from that message. (*Degradation* means "shame.")

> . . . the removal of the Indian tribes from the lands which they now occupy within the limits of the several states and Territories . . . is of . . . high importance to our Union, and may be accomplished . . . in a manner to promote the interest and happiness of those tribes. . . . For the removal of the tribes within the limits of the State of Georgia the motive has been peculiarly strong. . . . The removal of [these] tribes . . . would not only shield them from impending ruin, but promote their welfare and happiness. . . . [If this doesn't happen] their degradation and extermination will be inevitable.

Why did President Monroe call for the removal of the Cherokees from Georgia?

_____

_____

Document 2

Andrew Jackson became U.S. president in March 1829. But long before becoming president, Jackson was widely known throughout the United States. In 1796, he was elected as the first congressman from the new state of Tennessee. The next year, he was elected to the U.S. Senate. But Jackson earned his greatest fame as a military officer. General Andrew Jackson became a national hero in 1815. He commanded U.S. forces in the defeat of the British at the Battle of New Orleans. This was the final combat of the War of 1812. Several years later, Jackson's fame grew even more. He gained notice as he led U.S. troops against the Seminole Indians in Spanish-owned Florida. It's little wonder that he was elected U.S. president in 1828 in a landslide victory. He ran against the sitting president, John Quincy Adams. Jackson won more than twice the number of electoral votes as Adams did.

Jackson became U.S. president in 1829. Right away, he had to face the growing conflict between the state of Georgia and the Cherokee Indians who lived in that state. (This conflict is described in the Historical Background section on page 35.) The Cherokees appealed to President Jackson. They asked him to enforce the treaties and protect them from the demands of Georgia.

(continued)

DBQ 7: INDIAN REMOVAL: IS IT JUSTIFIED? CONTINUED

Jackson gave his first annual message to Congress on December 8, 1829. In it, he responded to the pleas from the Cherokees. Here are some excerpts from that message. (*Countenanced* means "accepted." *Emigrate* means "move from your lands." *Effecting* means "achieving.")

> I informed the Indians inhabiting parts of Georgia and Alabama that their attempt . . . would not be countenanced by [me], and advised them to emigrate beyond the Mississippi. . . .
>
> As a means to effecting this end, I suggest . . . setting apart an ample district west of the Mississippi . . . to be guaranteed to the Indian tribes as long as they shall occupy it.

Whose side in the argument did Jackson support, the Cherokees or Georgia?_____

_____

What solution to the conflict between the Cherokees and Georgia did President Jackson propose? _____

_____

_____

Document 3

The Cherokees now appealed to Congress. Surely, they hoped, Congress would uphold their rights. The Cherokees made their appeal to Congress in December 1829. Here are some excerpts from it. (*Inducements* means "attractions." *Encroachments* means "violations.")

> To the honorable . . . Senate and House of Representatives of the United States . . .
>
> [This] is the land of our nativity, and the land of our . . . birth. We cannot consent to abandon it, for another *far inferior,* and which holds out for us no inducements. We do, moreover, protest against the . . . measures of our neighbor, the state of Georgia, in her attempt to extend her laws over us . . . in direct opposition to treaties . . . of the United States. . . . To protect [us] from . . . these encroachments upon [our] rights, [we] earnestly pray [you].

(continued)

DBQ 7: INDIAN REMOVAL: IS IT JUSTIFIED? *CONTINUED*

What were the Cherokees asking Congress to do? _____

_____

_____

Document 4

In January 1830, at President Jackson's request, the Indian Removal Act was introduced into Congress. Here are sections of that act.

> . . . the President of the United States [may] cause . . . territory belonging to the United States, west of the river Mississippi, . . . to be divided into a suitable number of districts, for the reception of such tribes or nations of Indians as may choose to exchange the lands where they now reside, and remove there. . . .
>
> . . . in the making of any such exchange or exchanges . . . the President [shall] solemnly . . . assure the tribe or nation . . . that the United States will forever secure and guaranty to them, and their heirs or successors, the country so exchanged with them.

Summarize what the Indian Removal Act of 1830 said. _____

_____

_____

_____

Document 5

Like Jackson, Lewis Cass was a U.S. general in the War of 1812. He was then appointed governor of the Territory of Michigan. He held this post until 1831. Jackson admired Cass and later appointed him to his cabinet as secretary of war. Still later, Cass served as U.S. senator from Michigan after it became a state in 1837.

The following excerpts come from an article Cass wrote for a popular magazine in January of 1830. (*Barbarous* means "uncivilized and primitive." "The chase" refers to hunting.)

(continued)

39

DBQ 7: INDIAN REMOVAL: IS IT JUSTIFIED? *CONTINUED*

The destiny of the Indians, who inhabit the cultivated portions of the territory of the United States, . . . has long been a subject of debate. . . .

[They are a] barbarous people, depending for subsistence upon the scanty and precarious supplies furnished by the chase, [and] cannot live in contact with a civilized community. . . .

Let the offer of a new country be made to them with ample means to reach it and to subsist in it, with ample security for its peaceful and perpetual possession. . . .

Source: Lewis Cass, "Removal of the Indians," *North American Review,* January 1830.

Which side did Cass support, the Cherokees or the state of Georgia? _____

_____

Why, according to Cass, were the Cherokees (and other tribes living in the southeastern states), unable to live with success "in contact with a civilized community"? _____

_____

_____

_____

Document 6

Congress debated Indian removal in the late winter and early spring of 1830. Theodore Frelinghuysen was a U.S. senator from New Jersey. He was one of the senators who supported the cause of the Indians. He was opposed to the Indian Removal Act. He thought that the U.S. government (with President Jackson's approval) would trick, bribe, and bully the Indian tribes as it carried out the law. This trickery, he feared, would lure the Indians into selling their lands. They would accept wastelands in the West in the place of their fine lands in the South. Here are excerpts from a six-hour-long speech Frelinghuysen made during these debates. (*Cession* means "giving up." *Confiding* means "trusting." *Professions* means "declarations." *Importunity* means "repeated requests." *Cupidity* means "extreme greed.")

(continued)

DBQ 7: INDIAN REMOVAL: IS IT JUSTIFIED? *CONTINUED*

> God, in his providence, planted these tribes on this . . . continent.
>
> . . . we cannot rightfully complete the cession of [their] lands, or take them by violence, if [their] consent be withheld. . . .
>
> The confiding Indian [over many years] listened to our professions of friendship; we called him brother, and he believed us. Millions after millions he has yielded to our importunity, until we have acquired more than can be cultivated in centuries—and yet we crave more. We have crowded the tribes upon a few miserable acres [in our South]; it is all that is left to them of their once boundless forests: and still . . . our insatiated cupidity cries, Give! Give!

What, according to Senator Frelinghuysen, was the real reason why President Jackson wanted to relocate the Cherokees and other southeastern tribes west, beyond the Mississippi River? _____

_____

_____

_____

PART B   Essay: It's April 1830, and Congress is debating the Indian Removal Act. Should this law be passed? Write a newspaper editorial that expresses your opinion.

DBQ 8: HOW DID SLAVERY LEAD TO THE CIVIL WAR?

Historical Background

In colonial times, slavery of Africans existed in every American colony, North and South. The first arrival of African slaves into the colonies occurred in 1619. A Dutch ship brought twenty Africans to Virginia, where they were sold into slavery. Slavery gradually spread through all thirteen colonies. By 1776, almost 600,000 slaves lived in our country. This totaled almost 20 percent of the nation's population—one in every five people.

But the extent of America's slave population in 1776 was uneven. In many of the northern states, slaves made up less than 1 percent of the population. New York and New Jersey were the northern states with the largest number of slaves. Even there, slaves made up only about 7 percent of the total population. In the southern states, however, African slavery was more strongly rooted. In Virginia and South Carolina, slaves counted for close to 40 percent of the population. Slaves made up over 25 percent of the population in North Carolina, Maryland, and Georgia. So slavery existed all through the nation at the time of American independence. But it was largely confined to the South.

The American Revolution had a great impact on slavery in America. The Declaration of Independence stated that "all men are created equal." The Revolution itself was said to be a fight for freedom. Thoughtful Americans, North and South, found it difficult to square these ideals with the existence of slavery. During and soon after the Revolution, slavery came under attack. By 1800, all northern states had ended slavery or begun the process of ending it over time. Even in the South, many people began to question slavery. In the state legislatures of Maryland, Virginia, and Delaware, serious efforts were made to abolish slavery. But these efforts ultimately failed. No southern states put an end to slavery. Still, many southern leaders spoke out publicly about the injustices of slavery. These leaders included slave owners such as Thomas Jefferson and George Washington.

Many Southerners did see that slavery clashed with democratic ideals. But most white people in the South continued to support slavery. For some, there seemed no other choice. Slavery was, as Jefferson said, like "holding a wolf by the ears . . . we can neither hold him, nor safely let him go." For others, slavery was a basic economic need. The South had a farming economy. Slaves were needed to raise the cotton, tobacco, sugar cane, and other farm produce. Slavery was too strongly rooted in the South. Ending it seemed, for many, not possible.

By the late 1700s, slavery was dead or dying throughout the North. In the South, its support was growing stronger. For growing numbers of Southerners, an end to slavery was unthinkable. In 1790, Congressman St. George Tucker of South Carolina issued an ominous warning. Abolition of slavery, he said, " . . . [will] never be submitted to by the South without a civil war."

(continued)

DBQ 8: HOW DID SLAVERY LEAD TO THE CIVIL WAR? *CONTINUED*

■ **Directions:** The following question is based on the documents (1–7) that follow. Before reading these documents, be sure to

1. Carefully read and think about the document-based question that follows these directions.

2. Ask yourself: What do I already know about this question and its topic? What did I learn from reading the Historical Background section? If I had to answer the document-based question without reading any of the documents, what would I say?

3. Take a few minutes to jot down the major things you already know about this topic and question. What important names, dates, events, and major ideas do you already know?

4. Now read each document carefully. Ask yourself: How does this document help to answer the document-based question? Underline things of special importance and jot notes in the margins. If you're confused by or don't understand a document, go on to the next one. Later, if you have time, you can go back.

5. Develop a thesis statement that directly answers the document-based question. You'll want to state this thesis early in your essay.

6. Briefly outline your entire essay. Make sure that what you say in it supports and proves your thesis statement. In your essay, plan how you'll use the information found in the documents and what you know already about this topic.

7. Carefully write your essay. As you include supportive information from documents, be sure to cite the sources of this information. This will add authority and credibility to what you're saying.

Question: How did slavery grow to become the issue that, more than anything else, split the United States, North and South, causing secession and the Civil War?

PART A

The following documents will help you answer the document-based question. Read each document carefully. Answer the question or questions that follow each document.

(continued)

DBQ 8: HOW DID SLAVERY LEAD TO THE CIVIL WAR? *CONTINUED*

Document 1

As the U.S. population spread westward, new states asked to join the Union. This caused the divisive issue of slavery to rise again and again. Would slavery move west with new settlement? Would the number of slave states increase? Or would the South and its support of slavery slowly be outnumbered by the addition of new states that were free of slavery?

As years passed, the proposed addition of new states sparked anger and bitterness between the northern and southern states. In 1818, the Territory of Missouri asked to enter as a slave state. This request quickly became a crisis that threatened the unity of the nation. Slavery had existed in this area years before it became part of U.S. territory. But now Missouri sought statehood, and as a slave state. At this time, there were an equal number of slave and free states. With the addition of Missouri, the slave states would outnumber the free states in the U.S. Senate.

Many in Congress refused to allow the admission of Missouri as a slave state. New York Congressman James Tallmadge was one of these men. Tallmadge hated slavery. He proposed that Missouri be allowed to enter the union, but only if slavery were abolished there over a period of time. This "Tallmadge Amendment" passed the House of Representatives. Southern supporters of slavery sprang to the defense. For almost two years, a bitter and angry debate took place in Congress and all through the United States over slavery.

Former president Thomas Jefferson was now an old man nearing the age of eighty. He closely followed the Missouri debate in newspaper reports and in his own letters exchanged with political leaders. Years earlier, back in the 1780s, Jefferson had said of slavery, "I tremble for my country when I reflect that God is just . . . his justice cannot sleep forever." Now these fears seemed to be coming true. The crisis over slavery in Missouri seemed to threaten the unity of the nation. The following are excerpts from two letters Jefferson wrote to friends. (*Portentous* means "ominous and fearful.")

> The Missouri question is the most portentous one which ever threatened our Union. In the gloomiest moment of the Revolutionary War I never had any apprehensions equal to what I feel from this. . . .
> —letter to Hugh Nelson, February 1820
>
> But this momentous question, like a fire bell in the night, awakened and filled me with terror. I considered it at once as the knell* of the Union.
> —letter to John Holmes, April 1820

* Jefferson is referring to a death knell, which is an omen of death or a bell rung to signal a death.

(continued)

DBQ 8: HOW DID SLAVERY LEAD TO THE CIVIL WAR? CONTINUED

Why was Jefferson so frightened about the Missouri Compromise crisis? _____

_____

_____

Document 2

The political leaders of the South demanded over and over again that slavery be allowed to spread west. They wanted slavery in the new territories and states. The South tried to unite with the West for political purposes. Both regions were largely based on farming. So this alliance made sense. Also, as long as the alliance held, the people of the South felt secure on two counts. They felt that slavery would not be abolished where it existed. They also felt confident that slavery would spread west with the growth of new settlement.

Here are political maps showing the state votes for U.S. president in a series of elections between 1800 and 1860.

1800

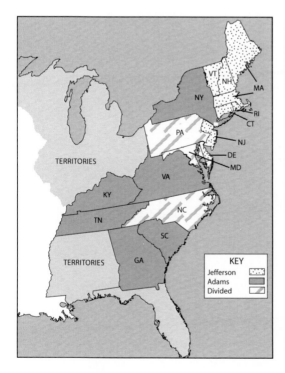

1828

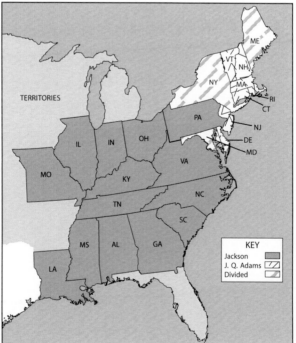

(continued)

DBQ 8: HOW DID SLAVERY LEAD TO THE CIVIL WAR? *CONTINUED*

1844

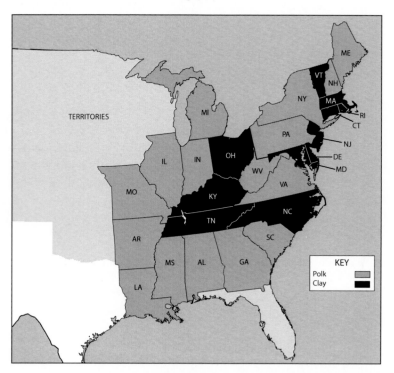

1856

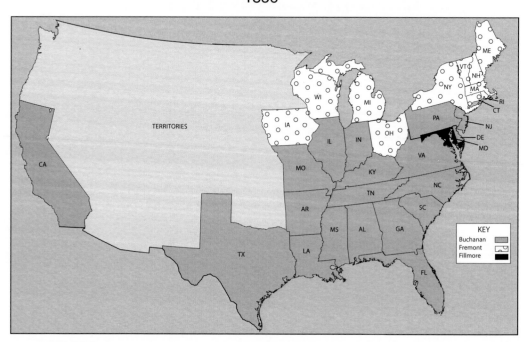

(continued)

DBQ 8: HOW DID SLAVERY LEAD TO THE CIVIL WAR? *CONTINUED*

1860

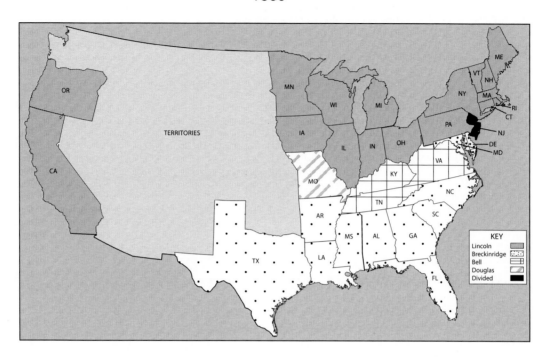

How was the result of the election of 1860 different from the earlier election results?

_____

_____

Why did the result of the election of 1860 frighten the South? _____

_____

_____

Document 3

For years, the Missouri Compromise of 1820 seemed to settle the issue of slavery. This law drew a line running from the southern state line of Missouri west into the territories. All areas to the north of this line were closed to slavery. Only those areas to the south of this line were open to any growth of slavery.

For over thirty years, an uneasy truce lasted. Then, in 1854, it ended. Senator Stephen Douglas, of Illinois, proposed a new law. It would open the Kansas and Nebraska territories to slavery if their residents voted for this. Both areas were north of the Missouri Compromise line.

(continued)

DBQ 8: HOW DID SLAVERY LEAD TO THE CIVIL WAR? CONTINUED

Quickly the Northern opponents of slavery joined together to condemn Douglas's Kansas-Nebraska Act. One of the leading opponents was Senator Salmon Chase of Ohio. He spoke out against the law on the floor of the U.S. Senate. Here is an excerpt from that speech.

> And what does slavery ask for now? . . . it demands that a time-honored and sacred agreement [the Missouri Compromise of 1820] be taken back. . . . [If this bill is passed into law, it will show] all thinking people that compromises with slavery will endure only as long as they serve the interests of slavery. It will convince them that the only safe and honorable ground for non-slaveholders to stand upon is that of restricting slavery within state limits and excluding it absolutely from all areas of federal jurisdiction [the Western territories].

Why did Chase (and many others) oppose passage of the Kansas-Nebraska Act?

_____

_____

What did Chase and other opponents of slavery learn from this crisis? _____

_____

_____

Document 4

In 1858, Abraham Lincoln ran for the U.S. Senate seat from Illinois. His opponent was Senator Stephen Douglas. Lincoln and Douglas traveled around the state debating major issues. They spoke in front of large crowds of interested citizens. On October 16 they met in Alton, a town in southern Illinois. It was not far from the city of St. Louis, Missouri. Lincoln said the following during that debate.

> I desire no concealment of my opinions in regard to the institution of slavery. I look upon it as a great evil . . . "A house divided against itself cannot stand." I believe this government [of the United States] cannot endure permanently half slave and half free. I do not expect the house to fall—but I do expect it will cease to be divided. It will become all one thing, or all the other.

(continued)

DBQ 8: HOW DID SLAVERY LEAD TO THE CIVIL WAR? *CONTINUED*

Lincoln took the "house divided" allusion from the Bible. In Matthew 12:25 Jesus said, "Every kingdom divided against itself is brought to desolation; and every city or house divided against itself shall not stand."

What was Lincoln's prediction for the future of the United States? _____

_____

_____

Document 5

Lincoln lost the 1858 U.S. Senate election to Stephen Douglas. But two years later, in 1860, he was nominated as the Republican Party's candidate for U.S. president. That year the Republican Party platform included this statement:

> . . . the normal condition of all the territory of the United States is that of freedom . . . we deny the authority of Congress, or a territorial legislature, or of any individuals to give legal existence to slavery in any territory of the United States.

What did Lincoln's Republican Party say about the possible expansion of slavery into the new western territories? _____

_____

_____

Document 6

On November 6, 1860, Abraham Lincoln was elected U.S. president. As you saw in Document 2, Lincoln's support was only in the North. He won no electoral votes in any southern slaveholding states. Six weeks after the election, South Carolina became the first of the southern states to leave the Union. South Carolina's leaders wrote and voted for a declaration of secession stating the reasons for this action. The declaration was modeled on the 1776 Declaration of Independence. Here are some excerpts from South Carolina's declaration.

(continued)

DBQ 8: HOW DID SLAVERY LEAD TO THE CIVIL WAR? *CONTINUED*

> . . . a geographic line has been drawn across the Union, and all the States north of that line have united in the election of a man [as] . . . President . . . whose opinions and purposes are hostile to Slavery . . . he has declared that . . . "Government cannot endure permanently half slave, half free."
>
> On the 4th of March next [the North] will take possession of the Government. It has announced that the South shall be excluded from the common territory . . . and that a war must be waged against Slavery until it shall cease throughout the United States.

What, according to the declaration of secession, did the 1860 election of Lincoln mean to South Carolina and the South? _____

_____

Document 7

On March 4, 1861, Abraham Lincoln became president of the United States. In the previous four months, seven southern states had seceded from the Union. They created the Confederate States of America. These Confederate states were South Carolina, Mississippi, Florida, Alabama, Georgia, Louisiana, and Texas. At his inauguration, Lincoln gave a firm but also calming and peaceful speech. He hoped that no war would break out. One very short part of his speech focused on the crux of the problem between North and South.

> One section of our country believes slavery is *right* and ought to be extended [into the territories], while the other believes it is *wrong* and ought not to be extended. This is the only substantial dispute.

What, according to Lincoln, was the only major issue between the northern and southern states? _____

_____

PART B Essay: How did slavery grow to become the issue that, more than anything else, split the United States, North and South, causing secession and the Civil War?

DBQ 9: WHY DID THE SOUTH LOSE THE CIVIL WAR?

Historical Background

All too often, the public responds to the outbreak of war with excitement, enthusiasm, and eagerness. This was the case in April of 1861 when the U.S. Civil War began. On both sides, North and South, bold newspaper headlines blared the news of the war's beginning. Instead of fear and worry, the public responded with bluster, bragging, and belligerence.

Events quickly followed the war's outbreak. In the next six weeks, four additional states left the Union. These new members of the Confederacy were Virginia, North Carolina, Arkansas, and Tennessee. In both the North and South, thousands of young men eagerly enlisted in a wave of patriotism. Within only weeks, vast armies of blue-coated Union soldiers and gray-coated Confederate solders faced one another. The United States began what became the bloodiest and most costly war in all of its history.

In those early days of the war, the Southerners were confident that their cause would prevail. Some of this confidence was simply bravado and enthusiasm. But much of it grew from a clear understanding of the facts. The South did have many advantages. Perhaps its greatest advantage was its situation. Its sole objective was independence. It simply had to defend itself, to hold out long enough to exhaust the patience and the will of the North. The South had other advantages, too. Almost all Confederate troops were country boys, used to working and living outdoors and skilled in the use of firearms. Also, the South was blessed with brilliant military leadership. Robert E. Lee and Thomas (Stonewall) Jackson were far more talented than most of the Union generals they faced. Finally, the South hoped that major European nations would support them in this conflict. Both England and France welcomed a fractured and weakened United States. If the South won, the United States would be a less important economic and political rival. Also, textile mills in England and France desperately needed the South's cotton. It's no wonder that 350,000 young men volunteered to serve the southern cause in the first month of the war. It's no wonder that they were so confident in the success of their cause.

Yet, four years later, the North had won. Much of the defeated South now lay in ruins. Only four years earlier, southern soldiers had been eager for war and confident of victory. Now most of those young men were dead or maimed. What had happened? Why did the South lose?

■ **Directions:** The following question is based on the documents (1–5) that follow. Before reading these documents, be sure to

    1. Carefully read and think about the document-based question that follows these directions.

    2. Ask yourself: What do I already know about this question and its topic? What did I learn from reading the Historical Background

(continued)

DBQ 9: WHY DID THE SOUTH LOSE THE CIVIL WAR? *CONTINUED*

section? If I had to answer the document-based question without reading any of the documents, what would I say?

3. Take a few minutes to jot down the major things you already know about this topic and question. What important names, dates, events, and major ideas do you already know?

4. Now read each document carefully. Ask yourself: How does this document help to answer the document-based question? Underline things of special importance and jot notes in the margins. If you're confused by or don't understand a document, go on to the next one. Later, if you have time, you can go back.

5. Develop a thesis statement that directly answers the document-based question. You'll want to state this thesis early in your essay.

6. Briefly outline your entire essay. Make sure that what you say in it supports and proves your thesis statement. In your essay, plan how you'll use the information found in the documents and what you already know about this topic.

7. Carefully write your essay. As you include supportive information from documents, be sure to cite the sources of this information. This will add authority and credibility to what you're saying.

Question: Why did the South lose the Civil War?

 PART A The following documents will help you answer the document-based question. Read each document carefully. Answer the question or questions that follow each document.

Document 1

The Civil War was one of the world's first modern wars. Factory-made products fueled the armies of both North and South. These included items such as rifles, pistols, artillery, uniforms, boots, blankets, medical supplies, iron-clad naval ships, railroads, and steam power. It took more than courage and determination to win the war. It took industrial might. This document shows how the North and South compared in measures of industrial strength.

(continued)

DBQ 9: WHY DID THE SOUTH LOSE THE CIVIL WAR? *CONTINUED*

	North	South
% of U.S. factory production	81%	19%
% of railroad mileage	66%	34%

Which side, North or South, was more industrialized? _____

How do you suppose industrial strength affected the outcome of the war?

_____

_____

Document 2

Fighting was gory. Both sides, North and South, suffered horrendous casualties. The violence of battle and the awful death rates that resulted made the Civil War the most costly of all U.S. wars. In all, over 600,000 men were killed outright or died of disease and wounds. (This almost equals the total American deaths in all other wars in our history, combined.) Another 400,000 were seriously wounded. Many were marked as Civil War veterans for the rest of their lives by their missing arms or legs. As the bloody fighting continued, from one awful battle to the next, both sides ran short of soldiers.

The following table shows the manpower counts, North and South, at the beginning of the War.

Population of North and South (1860)	
North	22 million
South	9 million (3.5 million of these were slaves)

Which side had the clear advantage of population?_____

Do you think that the 3.5 million slaves in the South were a military advantage or disadvantage for the Confederacy? Explain your reasoning. _____

_____

_____

(continued)

DBQ 9: WHY DID THE SOUTH LOSE THE CIVIL WAR? *CONTINUED*

Document 3

Because of its strong navy, the North was able to impose a blockade on the South. Over time, this blockade closed most southern ports to major imports and exports. As a result, the Union was able to cut off southern cotton exports to England and France. Both of those countries had hundreds of textile mills. These mills used southern cotton to make cloth and clothing. The Confederate government hoped that this cotton shortage would persuade England and France to help the South. Perhaps they would not become actual allies of the South. But at least they might put pressure on the North to end the war and grant the South its independence.

When the war broke out, European textile mills had an oversupply of cotton on hand. Painful shortages didn't really happen until 1863. Many mills were then forced to close, which caused rising unemployment. But both England and France soon began to relieve the shortage by importing cotton from Egypt and India.

During these same years, English farmers suffered several years of poor harvests. The results were high prices and food shortages. U.S. farmers from the North and West came to their aid. U.S. harvests increased, thanks to the new McCormick reaper. Rapid railroad transportation brought farm products quickly to U.S. ports, which the Union navy controlled. Ships rushed U.S. wheat, corn, and other food products to Europe. This table shows what happened to the production of American cotton, wheat, and corn during the Civil War. (Note that some data is unavailable.)

U.S. Farm Production, 1859–1865			
	Cotton	**Corn**	**Wheat**
1859	5,387,000 bales	539,000,000 bushels	173,000,000 bushels
1860	5,600,000 bales	600,000,000 bushels	170,000,000 bushels
1861	4,490,000 bales	NA	NA
1862	1,597,000 bales	NA	NA
1863	447,000 bales	NA	NA
1864	299,000 bales	NA	NA
1865	2,090,000 bales	731,000,000 bushels	170,000,000 bushels

NA = figures not available

Source: *Historical Statistical Abstract of the United States,* Colonial Times to 1970.

(continued)

DBQ 9: WHY DID THE SOUTH LOSE THE CIVIL WAR? *CONTINUED*

In the years just before the Civil War, England and France seemed to be tied by economics more to the South than to the North.

This document shows how and why these economic ties changed during the war. Explain. _____

_____

How did these economic changes affect the way that Europeans viewed the U.S. Civil War? _____

_____

Document 4

It's difficult to say how close Britain and France were to actually intervening in the Civil War on the side of the South. In mid-1862, the fortunes of war were running against the North. At this time, the French government made a proposal to British leaders. France suggested that the two countries help to mediate an end to the U.S. Civil War, allowing the Confederate states to become independent. Some British leaders favored the plan. But then President Lincoln did something that helped to turn public opinion in Britain and France against the South and toward the North. A modern historian explains this in the following excerpt from his biography of Abraham Lincoln. (The phrase "Lincoln's declaration of freedom" in the excerpt refers to the Emancipation Proclamation.)

> . . . immense throngs in London, Birmingham, and other British cities would rally to celebrate Lincoln's declaration of freedom and . . . public opinion would make it impossible for any British government to intervene on behalf of the slaveholding Confederacy. . . .

Source: *LINCOLN* by David Herbert Donald. (N.Y.: Simon and Schuster Adult Publishing Group, 1995.)

How did the Emancipation Proclamation turn British public opinion against the South?

_____

_____

_____

(continued)

Document-Based Assessment for U.S. History

DBQ 9: WHY DID THE SOUTH LOSE THE CIVIL WAR? *CONTINUED*

Document 5

The people who founded the Confederate States of America believed in the right of secession and states' rights. Indeed, the right of each state to resist the power of the national government was a basic philosophy of the South. Yet wars are waged best by countries whose people unite to accept and obey the rule of the national government and its commander-in-chief. Resistance to a central government's directing of the nation's armies and people weakens the war effort. States' rights may have undermined the South's war effort.

President Jefferson Davis was a fine man who worked very hard to serve the Confederacy and to win its war for independence. But he struggled greatly against many states' righters. Chief among these was Davis's own vice president, Alexander Stephens. These people opposed many of Davis's efforts to centralize control of the war. They especially resisted efforts to set up and enforce a draft law. The excerpt below is from a twentieth-century historian. He describes Davis's efforts and how fellow Confederates resisted and undermined them.

> . . . Davis sought to centralize power. The Southern states, however, had always been very conscious of states' rights and had often resisted the centralizing tendencies of the old government. The same impulses [toward centralization] in the new [Confederate] government were no more pleasing and even the necessities of war-making did not reconcile the new Confederacy to such concentration.
>
> Davis was bitterly opposed by powerful Governors in Georgia and North Carolina.

Source: Roy F. Nichols, *The Stakes of Power: 1845–1877,* Hill and Wang, 1961.

How was the South's war effort weakened by its own basic political beliefs? _____

_____

_____

PART B   Essay: Why did the South lose the Civil War?

DBQ 10: RECONSTRUCTION: A NOBLE EFFORT, OR OPPRESSION AND PUNISHMENT?

Historical Background

Few chapters in our nation's history are remembered with such anger and bitterness as is the period we know as Reconstruction. Reconstruction was the effort to bring peace to North and South and to reunite our nation at the conclusion of the Civil War. Making peace after any war is difficult. It's especially difficult after a civil war. It was probably inevitable that resentment and hatred resulted from the effort to reconstruct the nation after the horrific Civil War. But the scale of the ill feelings that grew from Reconstruction was remarkable. Even today, over 140 years after Reconstruction, the arguments continue.

Lincoln's assassination in April 1865 was a huge loss for those who hoped for a generous and welcoming reunion of North and South. Many northern political leaders wanted to punish the South and its "rebel" leaders harshly. Lincoln, though, was planning for a lenient peace. Only a few weeks before the war's end, in his Second Inaugural Address, Lincoln shared his vision for a lenient peace. He called on his fellow Northerners to join with him: "With malice toward none, with charity for all; . . . let us strive on to . . . bind up the nation's wounds. . . . "

A wave of public anger followed Lincoln's murder on April 14, 1865. This anger strengthened those who were calling for revenge against the South. The new president, Andrew Johnson, favored Lincoln's moderate approach toward the South. But the northern Republican majority in Congress soon took control of Reconstruction. Congress passed a series of harsh Reconstruction Acts in 1867. They were designed to force major changes on the South as requirements for rejoining the Union.

These new laws divided the South into five military districts. Union generals, supported by thousands of Union soldiers, governed each district. Each of the former Confederate states was required to grant former slaves the right to vote. At the same time, many whites were denied that right. Southern leaders protested that their states were being unfairly punished. One reply to the South's protests came from Thaddeus Stevens, a Republican congressman from Pennsylvania. He justified the demand to give the vote to the freedmen (the newly freed slaves) in a speech in the House of Representatives. In that speech he said, "I am for Negro suffrage [the right to vote] in every rebel state. If it be just, it should not be denied; if it be necessary, it should be adopted; if it be a punishment to traitors, they deserve it."

Was granting the vote to the freed slaves part of Lincoln's plans? We'll never know for sure. But from what he said and wrote during the war, it appears that he wanted to give voting rights to at least some of the freed slaves. This would include ex-slaves who were educated and those who had fought in the war on the Union side. As Lincoln said in a letter to General James Wadsworth in January 1864, "The restoration of the Rebel States to the Union must rest upon the principle of civil and political equality of both races."

(continued)

57

DBQ 10: RECONSTRUCTION: A NOBLE EFFORT, OR OPPRESSION AND PUNISHMENT? *CONTINUED*

Even today historians debate why some Republicans demanded the right to vote for former slaves in the South. What were the true motives and objectives of these men? Were the Republican members of Congress sincere in their belief that the freed slaves should have full political rights, including the right to vote? Or did they want to use the ballots of the freed slaves to maintain political control of the southern states? (This would also preserve Republican control of the national government.) Did they figure that the new black voters would vote for the party — the Republicans — that got them the vote? Or did the Radical Republicans simply impose this requirement on the South as a way to humble and punish the former rebels? You study the evidence, and you decide.

■ **Directions:** The following question is based on the documents (1–6) that follow. Before reading these documents, be sure to

1. Carefully read and think about the document-based question that follows these directions.

2. Ask yourself: What do I already know about this question and its topic? What did I learn from reading the Historical Background section? If I had to answer the document-based question without reading any of the documents, what would I say?

3. Take a few minutes to jot down the major things you already know about this topic and question. What important dates, events, and major ideas do you already know?

4. Now read each document carefully. Ask yourself: How does this document help to answer the document-based question? Underline things of special importance and jot notes in the margins. If you're confused by or don't understand a document, go on to the next one. Later, if you have time, you can go back.

5. Develop a thesis statement that directly answers the document-based question. You'll want to state this thesis early in your essay.

6. Briefly outline your entire essay. Make sure that what you say in it supports and proves your thesis statement. In your essay, plan how you'll use the information found in the documents and what you know already about this topic.

7. Carefully write your essay. As you include supportive information from documents, be sure to cite the sources of this information. This will add authority and credibility to what you're saying.

Question: Why did the Reconstruction policies imposed on the South by the Republican-controlled Congress include the requirement that freed slaves be granted the right to vote?

(continued)

DBQ 10: RECONSTRUCTION: A NOBLE EFFORT, OR OPPRESSION AND PUNISHMENT? *CONTINUED*

PART A

The following documents will help you answer the document-based question. Read each document carefully. Answer the question or questions that follow each document.

Document 1

Six months before the end of the Civil War, a convention of northern black leaders met in Syracuse, New York. They knew the war was coming to an end. The slaves in the South would soon be released from bondage. These black leaders met in order to provide Congress with clear advice about the future of the newly freed slaves. The following are excerpts from their proclamation. (*Entreat* means "plead." *Franchise* means "right to vote." *Vigilance* means "watchfulness." *Enmity* means "hatred.")

> Fellow-citizens, let us entreat you, have faith in your own principles.
>
> If freedom is good for any, it is good for all. If you need the elective franchise, we need it even more. You are strong, we are weak; you are many, we are few; you are protected, we are exposed. Protect us with this safeguard of our liberty. . . .
>
> . . . give the elective franchise to every colored man of the South and you have at once four millions of friends who will guard with their vigilance, and if need be, defend with their arms, the . . . Federal Liberty from the treason and pollution of her enemies. You are sure of the enmity of the masters, — make sure of the friendship of the slaves; for, depend upon it, your Government cannot afford to encounter the enmity of both.

Source: Proceedings of the National Convention of Colored Men Held in Syracuse, New York, October 4–7, 1864.

Why, according to this proclamation, should Congress grant the right to vote to the newly freed slaves? _____

_____

_____

_____

(continued)

DBQ 10: RECONSTRUCTION: A NOBLE EFFORT, OR OPPRESSION AND PUNISHMENT? *CONTINUED*

Document 2

Southern black leaders also made appeals to Congress. In August 1865, four months after the war's end, a convention of freed former slaves met in Alexandria, Virginia. The following excerpt is from a proclamation issued by the convention.

> We warn you . . . that our only safety is in keeping [our enemies in the South] under . . . the military . . . until you have so amended the Federal Constitution that it will prohibit the States from [discriminating against us] on account of race or color. In one word, the only salvation for us besides the power of the Government, is in the *possession of the ballot*. Give us this, and we will protect ourselves.

Source: Convention of Colored Citizens of the State of Virginia, meeting in Alexandria, Virginia, August 2–5, 1865.

Why, according to this proclamation, did ex-slaves in the South need to have their right to vote protected and guaranteed? _____

_____

_____

Document 3

Pennsylvania Congressman Thaddeus Stevens was a firm, uncompromising supporter of the South's former slaves. Before the Civil War, he had been a fervent opponent of slavery. Like Lincoln, he joined the Republican Party in the 1850s. Both men agreed with the party's opposition to the spread of slavery into the western territories. But unlike Lincoln, Stevens had been an abolitionist. He had strongly believed in putting an end to slavery all through the United States. When he died in 1868, his gravestone was engraved, "Equality of Man Before His Creator."

The following excerpts come from a speech Stevens gave in the U.S. House of Representatives in January of 1867. In this speech, he explained why he supported forcing the southern states to grant the vote to the freed slaves. (*Ascendancy* means "dominance." *Avow* means "admit" or "announce." By "the Union Party," Stevens is referring to the Republican Party.)

(continued)

DBQ 10: RECONSTRUCTION: A NOBLE EFFORT, OR OPPRESSION AND PUNISHMENT? *CONTINUED*

> In the first place, it is just. . . . Have not loyal blacks as good a right to choose rulers and make laws as rebel whites?
>
> In the second place, it is a necessity in order to protect the loyal white men in the seceded states. The white Union men are in a great minority in each of those states. With them the blacks would . . . form a majority, control the states, and protect themselves.
>
> Another good reason is that it would insure the ascendancy of the Union Party. "Do [I] avow to a party purpose?"
>
> I do. For I believe . . . that . . . on the continued rise of [the Republican] party depends the safety of this great nation.

What reasons does Congressman Stevens identify for forcing the South to grant the vote to the former slaves? _____

_____

Document 4

In April 1861, when the Civil War first broke out, Andrew Johnson had been a U.S. senator from Tennessee. He was also a member of the Democratic Party. He opposed secession and remained loyal to the Union after Tennessee seceded. For this, he earned Lincoln's respect and gratitude. Three years later, Johnson ran as Lincoln's vice presidential candidate in the election of 1864. When Lincoln was killed, Johnson became president. He had been vice president for only a few weeks.

Johnson opposed the Radical Republicans who controlled Congress. He wanted the South to be reunited quickly with the North. He looked forward to the Democratic Party winning control of Congress. He also opposed the Republicans' efforts to give the former slaves the right to vote. The following excerpt is from Johnson's State of the Union message to Congress of December 1867. (*Manifestly* means "obviously." *Disfranchise* means "deny the right to vote to.")

(continued)

 Document-Based Assessment for U.S. History

Name _____   Date _____

> I would be unfaithful to my duty if I did not recommend the repeal of the acts of Congress which place . . . the Southern States under the domination of military masters.
>
> It is manifestly . . . the object of these laws to confer upon negroes the privilege of voting and to disfranchise such a number of white citizens as will give the former a clear majority at all elections in the Southern States. . . .

Why, according to President Johnson, did the Radical Republican leaders of Congress want the former slaves to have the power to vote? _____

_____

_____

Document 5

When Republican congressional leaders demanded voting rights for the newly freed slaves, people wondered about their motives. In the many years since the end of Reconstruction, historians have continued to examine their motives. One of those historians was William A. Dunning. He was a professor at Columbia University in New York City for many years until his death in 1922. The following excerpts come from a collection of his essays published in 1897.

> Four important [Northern] states Ohio, Michigan, Minnesota, and Kansas, had refused to extend the right of voting to the blacks, while [supporting] the Congressional policy of reconstruction. . . .
>
> [The motive of Congress was] to maintain Northern and Republican control through negro suffrage.

Source: William Archibald Dunning, *Essays on the Civil War and Reconstruction*, Macmillan Company, 1897.

Professor Dunning implied that the congressional Republicans were hypocrites. He suggested that they falsely acted as though they believed in racial justice, equal rights, and voting rights for the southern blacks. What made him see their actions as hypocritical? _____

_____

_____

(continued)

DBQ 10: RECONSTRUCTION: A NOBLE EFFORT, OR OPPRESSION AND PUNISHMENT? *CONTINUED*

What, according to Professor Dunning, were the real reasons why the congressional Republicans gave the right to vote to the newly freed slaves in the South?

_____

_____

Document 6

Kenneth M. Stampp was professor of history at the University of California at Berkeley from 1946 until 1983. Professor Stampp understood that the congressional Republicans had mixed reasons for supporting voting rights for the southern ex-slaves. But he believed that their motive was, in large part, sincere idealism. As he points out, many of these congressmen had been champions of abolition and human rights for years, long before the Civil War. The following excerpt is from Stampp's 1965 book about Reconstruction.

> [The pleas of the Congressional Republicans] for justice for the Negro, [and] their objections to [President] Johnson . . . on the ground that the Black Codes were restoring a form of slavery, cannot be discounted as hypocrisy. [Their motives grew, in part, from] the moral idealism that they inherited from the abolitionists.

Source: Kenneth M. Stampp, *The Era of Reconstruction, 1865–1877*, Random House, 1965.

How did Professor Stampp see the motives of the congressional Republicans differently from the way Professor Dunning viewed them? _____

_____

_____

PART B Essay: Why did the Reconstruction policies imposed on the South by the Republican-controlled Congress include the requirement that freed slaves be granted the right to vote?

DBQ 11: HOW DID THE UNITED STATES CHANGE IN THE DECADES AFTER THE CIVIL WAR?

Historical Background

Tremendous changes occurred in the United States during the decades following the Civil War. The war itself was the cause of some of these changes. Six hundred thousand young men had died. Hundreds of thousands more had been severely wounded. These deaths and injuries affected every village, town, and city in our country. Cities, railroads, factories, farms, and ways of earning a living had been destroyed. This was especially true in the South, where most of the fighting had occurred. These effects of the war left long-lasting scars on our nation. It required decades to repair the damage.

Other changes had their origin in the politics of the Civil War. In 1860, Abraham Lincoln was elected president, and the southern states seceded. As a result, the Republican Party had control of the national government. This allowed the passage of a number of laws with far-reaching effects. In 1862, Congress passed the Homestead Act. This law offered free 160-acre plots in the West to anyone over the age of twenty-one. The offer was open to men, to women, and to people of any race or national origin. Almost right away, land-hungry families streamed west. By the year 1900, more than 80 million acres in the West were turned into farms. This was an area greater in size than all six New England states.

Another law passed in the same year as the Homestead Act also had a transforming effect on the nation. This was the Pacific Railway Act of 1862. It authorized the building of a transcontinental (cross-country) railroad, linking the east and west coasts of the United States. Only four years after the war's end, the railroad was completed. This was followed by other lines reaching across the western prairies and over the Rockies. By 1900, five east-west lines spanned the continent, with a web of interconnecting lines.

Many other changes of the post–Civil War decades simply continued trends already begun. The pace of industrial growth increased. This drew more people from the American farms to the factories. In turn, smog-filled, crowded cities grew. The factory jobs also lured workers from European farms. Immigrants poured into the United States by the millions.

All these changes swept across the United States between 1860 and 1900. They were transforming. The early America of quiet farms had become a modern America of noise, factories, and cities.

■ **Directions:** The following question is based on the documents (1–5) that follow. Before reading these documents, be sure to

　　　　1. Carefully read and think about the document-based question that follows these directions.

(continued)

DBQ 11: HOW DID THE UNITED STATES CHANGE IN THE DECADES AFTER THE CIVIL WAR? *CONTINUED*

2. Ask yourself: What do I already know about this question and its topic? What did I learn from reading the Historical Background section? If I had to answer the document-based question without reading any of the documents, what would I say?

3. Take a few minutes to jot down the major things you already know about this topic and question. What important names, dates, events, and major ideas do you already know?

4. Now read each document carefully. Ask yourself: How does this document help to answer the document-based question? Underline things of special importance and jot notes in the margin. If you're confused by or don't understand a document, go on to the next one. Later, if you have time, you can go back.

5. Develop a thesis statement that directly answers the document-based question. You'll want to state this thesis early in your essay.

6. Briefly outline your entire essay. Make sure that what you say in it supports and proves your thesis statement. In your essay, plan how you'll use the information found in the documents and what you know already about this topic.

7. Carefully write your essay. As you include supportive information from documents, be sure to cite the sources of this information. This will add authority and credibility to what you're saying.

Question: How did the United States change in the decades after the Civil War, between 1865 and 1900?

PART A The following documents discuss various changes which occurred in the United States during the decades following the Civil War. Examine each document carefully, and answer the question or questions that follow.

Document 1

The United States grew tremendously in the forty years between 1860 and 1900.

(continued)

DBQ 11: HOW DID THE UNITED STATES CHANGE IN THE DECADES AFTER THE CIVIL WAR? *CONTINUED*

1860 Population 31.4 million (34 states)

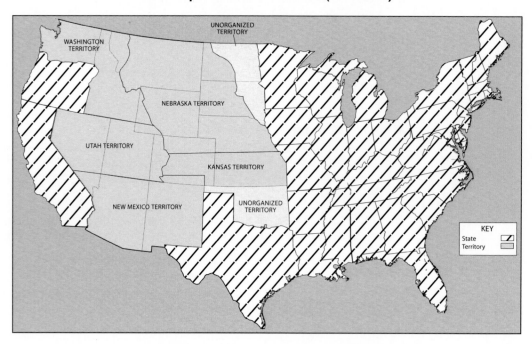

1900 Population 76 million (45 states)

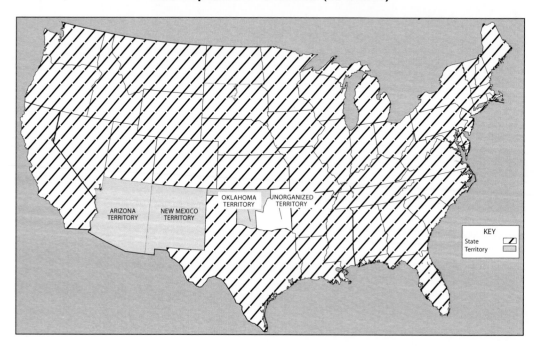

(continued)

DBQ 11: HOW DID THE UNITED STATES CHANGE IN THE DECADES AFTER THE CIVIL WAR? *CONTINUED*

How did the population and settlement pattern of the United States change between 1860 and 1900? _____

_____

Document 2

Major changes occurred in our nation's economic life.

U.S. Economic Changes			
	1860	**1900**	**Percentage Change**
Miles of RR track	30,000	195,000	+550%
Steel Production	13,000 tons	12,500,000 tons	+96,000%
Wheat Production	170 million bushels	600 million bushel	+253%
Corn Production	600 million bushels	2,600 million bushels	+333%
Cotton Production	5.6 million bales	10.1 million bales	+80%
Employment			
	1860	**1900**	**Percentage Change**
Farm	6.2 million	10.9 million	+75%
Nonfarm	4.3 million	18.2 million	+323%

As you can see, U.S. economic production increased greatly between 1860 and 1900. Using these data, identify several other patterns of economic change during this forty-year period. _____

_____

_____

(continued)

DBQ 11: HOW DID THE UNITED STATES CHANGE IN THE DECADES AFTER THE CIVIL WAR? *CONTINUED*

Document 3

The growing number of factory jobs drew people from rural farming areas into urban areas.

U.S. Urbanization			
	1860	**1900**	**% Change**
Rural Population	21 million	46 million	+119%
Urban Population	10.5 million	30 million	+186%

U.S. Cities, 1860

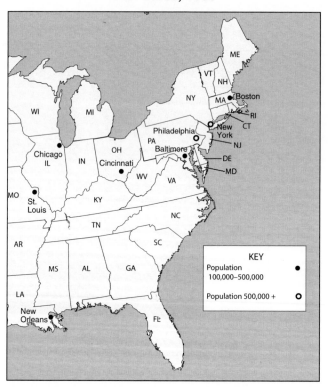

(continued)

DBQ 11: HOW DID THE UNITED STATES CHANGE IN THE DECADES AFTER THE CIVIL WAR? *CONTINUED*

U.S. Cities, 1900

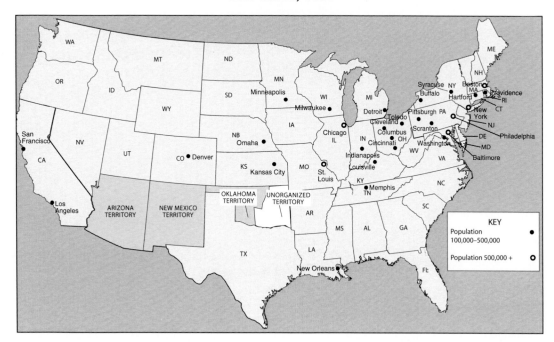

What changes in population patterns from 1860 to 1900 do the data in Document 3 show? _____

_____

_____

Document 4

Some economic regions prospered in the years following the Civil War. Other areas declined in wealth.

(continued)

Document-Based Assessment for U.S. History

DBQ 11: HOW DID THE UNITED STATES CHANGE IN THE DECADES AFTER THE CIVIL WAR? *CONTINUED*

Ten States with Greatest per Capita Wealth in 1860

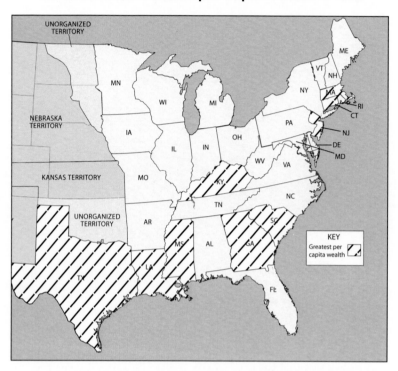

Ten States with Greatest per Capita Wealth in 1900

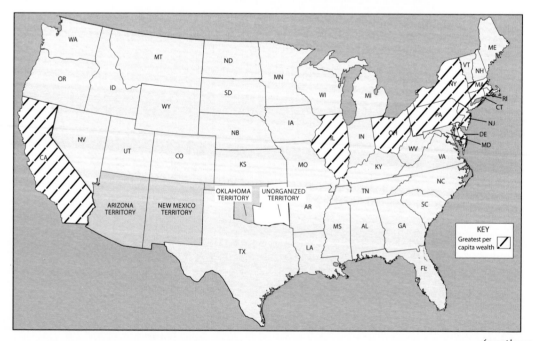

(continued)

DBQ 11: HOW DID THE UNITED STATES CHANGE IN THE DECADES AFTER THE CIVIL WAR? *CONTINUED*

Which region of the United States declined in comparative wealth between 1860 and 1900? Which region or regions became wealthier? _____

_____

_____

What do you think caused this major change in the wealth of regions?_____

_____

_____

_____

Document 5

Many immigrants came to the United States in the decades after the Civil War.

Foreign-Born Population of the United States	
1860	**1900**
4.1 million	10.3 million

How did the foreign-born population of the United States change between 1860 and 1900? _____

Why were so many immigrants coming to the United States? _____

_____

_____

PART B Essay: How did the United States change in the decades after the Civil War, between 1865 and 1900?

DBQ 12: SHOULD FURTHER IMMIGRATION TO THE UNITED STATES BE RESTRICTED?

This DBQ asks you to be part of history. It asks you to experience an episode in our history from the viewpoints of the people who took part in it. As you complete this DBQ essay, imagine that you are living in the 1890s. Those who actually lived at that time and who took part in this episode of history didn't know how it would all turn out. Imagine that you don't know, either. Use only information from the documents and from your outside learning about this subject up to the year 1900.

Historical Background

All of us who call ourselves Americans are either immigrants or the descendents of immigrants. People from Europe first came to North and South America about 500 years ago. They found Native Americans living here, whom they called Indians. But scientists tell us that even the Indians were the descendents of prehistoric Asian immigrants. They were hunters who walked to North America about 20,000 years ago. They used an ancient land bridge that connected North America and Asia at that time. (Other prehistoric Americans may have crossed the ocean to get here.) Most immigrants came to America of their own free will, many eagerly. Some, including all African slaves, were forced to come. But our ancestors all came here from other lands. The United States is a land of immigrants.

Through most of U.S. history, new immigrants have been welcomed. In fact, they often have been actively recruited. This was because of a simple ratio that has characterized the United States through most of its history. The nation had a lot of empty land and a chronic shortage of workers. This has typically made land cheap and labor expensive. It's no wonder that colonial tobacco farmers were so eager to acquire indentured servants from England or slaves from Africa. Or that colonial governments advertised for settlers, providing inexpensive or free lands. Or that the builders of the transcontinental railroad hired so many Chinese and Irish workers. Or that the Homestead Act of 1862 purposefully applied to U.S. citizens and to noncitizens alike. (As you remember, this law gave away millions of acres of free farmland in the West.) In fact, as the years passed, the United States became known and respected as a nation that welcomed new immigrants.

In the 1880s, the people of France wanted to honor the one-hundredth anniversary of both American independence and of their own revolution. They gave the American people the Statue of Liberty. It came to symbolize America's open door to the world's immigrants. At the statue's dedication ceremony in 1886, a plaque was laid at its base. On that plaque is engraved a poem by Emma Lazarus. She herself was an American immigrant from Russia. It reads:

(continued)

DBQ 12: SHOULD FURTHER IMMIGRATION TO THE UNITED STATES BE RESTRICTED? *CONTINUED*

> " . . . Give me your tired, your poor,
>
> Your huddled masses yearning to breathe free,
>
> The wretched refuse of your teeming shore.
>
> Send these, the homeless, tempest-tost to me,
>
> I lift my lamp beside the golden door!"

At times in U.S. history, however, our "golden door" has not been so welcoming. At times, Americans have feared and opposed immigration. At these times nativism (anti-immigrant feelings) becomes widespread. Nativist groups organize to try to limit immigration. Nativist feelings have often been strong when the pace of immigration has been especially fast. Strong nativism has also arisen when new immigrants seemed different, more foreign and alien than before. Nativism has often also flourished during economic bad times. Unemployed American workers have become resentful of competition from immigrants. The 1890s was one of those times when public opposition to immigration became especially strong.

Nativists in the 1890s worked to limit the number of immigrants entering the United States. They lobbied Congress for laws that would forbid all nonliterate immigrants from entering. (A nonliterate person is someone who cannot read or write.) Those who were uneducated would be denied entry. Immigrants are typically poor people. They are seeking better lives and greater chances for themselves and their children. In the 1890s, many came from countries where they had no opportunity for education. A great many of them could neither read nor write. So a literacy law would bar many immigrants from entering the United States.

Imagine that you are a newspaper editor. You're planning an editorial on the topic of future immigration. Should the U.S. "golden door" remain open? Or should the United States begin to restrict and limit future immigration by allowing entry only to those who are educated?

(continued)

DBQ 12: SHOULD FURTHER IMMIGRATION TO THE UNITED STATES BE RESTRICTED? *CONTINUED*

■ **Directions:** The following question is based on the documents (1–7) that follow. Before reading these documents, be sure to

1. Carefully read and think about the document-based question that follows these directions.

2. Ask yourself: What do I already know about this question and its topic? What did I learn from reading the Historical Background section? If I had to answer the document-based question without reading any of the documents, what would I say?

3. Take a few minutes to jot down the major things you already know about this topic and question. What important names, dates, events, and major ideas do you already know?

4. Now read each document carefully. Ask yourself: How does this document help to answer the document-based question? Underline things of special importance and jot notes in the margins. If you're confused by or don't understand a document, go on to the next one. Later, if you have time, you can go back.

5. Develop a thesis statement that directly answers the document-based question. You'll want to state this thesis early in your essay.

6. Briefly outline your entire essay. Make sure that what you say in it supports and proves your thesis statement. In your essay, plan how you'll use the information found in the documents and what you know already about this topic.

7. Carefully write your essay. As you include supportive information from documents, be sure to cite the sources of this information. This will add authority and credibility to what you're saying.

> **Question: Should the U.S. "golden door" remain open? Or should the United States restrict and limit future immigration by allowing entry only to those who are educated?**

PART A The following documents address various arguments made in support of, or in opposition to, restricting immigration in the late 1800s. Examine each document carefully, and answer the question or questions that follow.

(continued)

DBQ 12: SHOULD FURTHER IMMIGRATION TO THE UNITED STATES BE RESTRICTED? *CONTINUED*

Document 1

The nature of immigration to the United States changed greatly during the second half of the 1800s. The pace of immigration grew rapidly. The total number of immigrants arriving during any ten-year period didn't rise above one million until the 1840s. Four decades later, that number was over five million. By the 1890s, poor immigrants were crowding into the rapidly growing cities of the United States, creating slums. Italians made up 75 percent of New York City's construction workers. Polish and Russian Jews dominated that city's garment trades. By the 1890s, Chicago was the third largest "German city" in the world. (Only Berlin and Hamburg, in Germany, had more Germans.) Chicago was also the third largest "Norwegian city" in the world. (Only Oslo and Bergen, in Norway, had more Norwegians.) Sixty percent of Pennsylvania's coal miners were foreign-born. Immigrant populations were very large, especially in cities. Many Americans began to feel like strangers in their own country.

Not only did the pace of immigration change but so did the nature of the immigration. Earlier immigrants to the United States had come mostly from western and northern Europe. Most of those people had been English-speaking and Protestant. But by the late 1800s huge numbers of immigrants were arriving from countries in eastern and southern Europe. This included nations such as Russia, Poland, and Italy. Many other immigrants were coming from Asia, especially from China. Few of these new immigrants spoke English. Many were members of Catholic, Jewish, Eastern Orthodox, or members of other non-Protestant religions. These other faiths seemed strange and threatening to many Americans.

The following charts and tables show these changes to American immigration

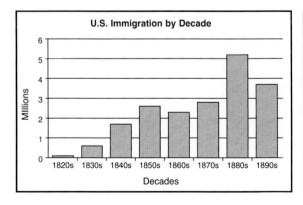

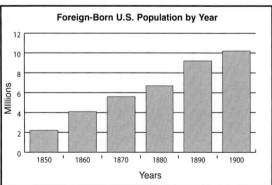

(continued)

DBQ 12: SHOULD FURTHER IMMIGRATION TO THE UNITED STATES BE RESTRICTED? *CONTINUED*

Sources of U.S. Immigration, 1820–1840

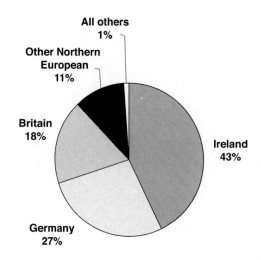

Sources of U.S. Immigration, 1860–1900

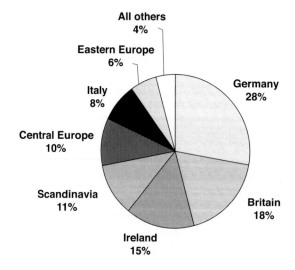

(continued)

DBQ 12: SHOULD FURTHER IMMIGRATION TO THE UNITED STATES BE RESTRICTED? *CONTINUED*

Number of Foreign-Born Americans by Country

1850

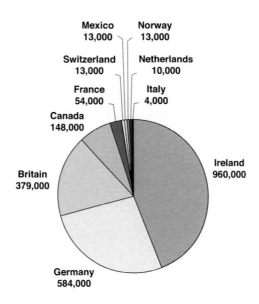

1900

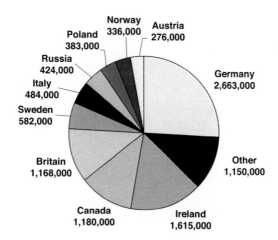

What do these tables and charts tell you about how American immigration changed in the late 1800s? _____

_____

_____

(continued)

Document-Based Assessment for
U.S. History

DBQ 12: SHOULD FURTHER IMMIGRATION TO THE UNITED STATES BE RESTRICTED? *CONTINUED*

Document 2

Reverend Josiah Strong was a very popular speaker and writer in the late nineteenth and early twentieth centuries. He was also a Protestant minister. His most famous book, *Our Country,* was published in 1885. It quickly became a best-seller. The following excerpts are from that book. (*Conspicuous* means "clearly visible.")

> . . . our . . . foreign [population] . . . is sadly conspicuous in our criminal records. This element constituted in 1870 twenty per cent of the population of New England, and furnishes seventy-five per cent of the crime.
>
> . . . our safety demands the assimilation of these strange populations, and the process of assimilation will become slower and more difficult as the population of foreigners increases.

Source: Josiah Strong, *Our Country: Its Possible Future and Its Present Crisis,* Baker & Taylor, 1885.

Why did Josiah Strong fear and oppose unrestricted immigration? _____

_____

_____

Document 3

In the years right after the Civil War, many people on the West Coast grew fearful about the large influx of immigrants from China. Before the war, hardly any Asians lived in the United States. By 1880, the nation had over 100,000 Asian immigrants. Anti-Chinese public opinion grew. It led Congress to pass the Chinese Exclusion Act of 1882. This law ended further immigration from China for ten years. Nine years later, the law was about to expire. Congress appointed a committee to study the issue and to give advice about whether to extend the law. The following are excerpts from that committee's report. (*Inimical* means "hostile.")

(continued)

DBQ 12: SHOULD FURTHER IMMIGRATION TO THE UNITED STATES BE RESTRICTED? *CONTINUED*

"U.S. Congress—House of Representatives—Report of the Select Committee on Immigration"

> There is urgent necessity for prompt legislation on the subject of Chinese immigration . . . [If we fail to re-enact the Chinese Exclusion Act] there will be no law to prevent the Chinese hordes from invading our country.
>
> Their [Chinese immigrants'] presence here is inimical to our institutions and is deemed injurious and a source of danger. They are a distinct race . . . they have no attachment to our country, its laws or its institutions, nor are they interested in its prosperity. They never assimilate with our people, our manners, tastes, religion, or ideas. With us they have nothing in common.

Source: "Report of the Select Committee on Immigration," Fifty-Second Congress, First Session.

As you can probably tell, the committee recommended making the law permanent. What reasons did it cite for doing this? _____

_____

_____

Document 4

Many labor union leaders feared immigration. They believed that it was forcing down wages for all workers. But some labor leaders spoke out against restricting immigration. Joseph McDonnell, himself an Irish immigrant, was one of these leaders. Here are excerpts from a newspaper editorial he wrote defending Chinese immigration. (*Tocsin* means "alarm.")

> The cry that "the Chinese must go" is both narrow and unjust. . . . It is merely a repetition of the cry that was raised years ago by . . . Americans against the immigration of Irishmen, Englishmen, Germans and others. . . . It now ill becomes those, or the descendants of those, against whom this cry was raised in past years, to raise a similar tocsin against a class of foreigners who have been degraded by ages of oppression.

Source: Unsigned editorial, "'The Chinese Must Go,'" (New York) *Labor Standard,* June 30, 1878.

(continued)

Document-Based Assessment for U.S. History

DBQ 12: SHOULD FURTHER IMMIGRATION TO THE UNITED STATES BE RESTRICTED? *CONTINUED*

Why did McDonnell criticize those who were demanding that "the Chinese must go"?

_____

_____

Document 5

Henry Cabot Lodge represented Massachusetts in the U.S. Congress for thirty-seven years. He served in the House of Representatives from 1887 to 1893. Then he served in the Senate from 1893 until his death in 1924. He was a Republican party leader and a close friend of Theodore Roosevelt. He was also a direct descendent of early Puritan founders of New England. Lodge feared that the large immigration threatened the United States and the purity of "the American race." He was especially concerned about immigrants from Italy, Poland, and other eastern and southern European countries. Here are some excerpts from a speech he made in Congress in 1896. In it, he called for laws restricting future immigration. (*Kindred people* means "people like us." *Peril* means "danger." *Portals* means "doorways.")

> The injury of unrestricted immigration to American wages and American standards of living is sufficiently plain and is bad enough, but the danger which this immigration threatens to the quality of our citizenship is far worse.
>
> The additions in this country until the present time have been from kindred people or from those with whom we have been long allied and who speak the same language.
>
> . . . it is on the moral qualities of the English-speaking race that our history, our victories, and all of our future rest. . . . If a lower race mixes with a higher in sufficient numbers, history teaches us that the lower race will prevail. . . . The lowering of a great race means not only its own decline but that of human civilization.
>
> There lies the peril at the portals of our land; there is pressing the tide of unrestricted immigration.

Why did Senator Lodge oppose and fear unrestricted immigration?_____

_____

_____

(continued)

DBQ 12: SHOULD FURTHER IMMIGRATION TO THE UNITED STATES BE RESTRICTED? *CONTINUED*

Document 6

Several large nativist organizations were popular in the 1890s. One was the American Protective Association. Another was the Immigration Restriction League. Both groups attracted thousands of members. Many were affluent, educated, and prominent citizens. Many who joined these groups feared that immigrants were to blame for labor union strikes and violence. They feared that immigrants brought with them from Europe dangerous ideas about socialism and communism. Many also feared the large numbers of Catholic immigrants who were arriving from Italy, Poland, and Germany. Nativists feared Catholics would blindly follow the orders of the pope, the head of their church. So nativists saw Catholics as a danger to democracy.

Here are excerpts from the oath of membership that was required of those who joined the American Protective Association.

> I do most solemnly promise and swear . . . that I will use my utmost power to strike the shackles and chains of blind obedience to the Roman Catholic church from the . . . consciences of a priest-ridden and church-oppressed people. . . .
>
> I furthermore promise and swear that . . . I will not vote for . . . any Roman Catholic, but will vote only for a Protestant.

The members of the American Protective Association were probably most opposed to immigration from which European countries? Why? _____

_____

_____

Document 7

In 1897, Congress passed a law limiting future immigration. This law stated that only prospective immigrants who could read and write would be allowed to come to the United States. All others would be refused. Senator Henry Cabot Lodge sponsored this law. He said:

> If we care for the welfare, the wages, or the standard of life of American workingmen, we should take immediate steps to limit foreign immigration. There is no danger . . . from the coming of skilled workers or of trained and educated men. But there is a serious danger from the flood of unskilled, ignorant foreign labor.

(continued)

DBQ 12: SHOULD FURTHER IMMIGRATION TO THE UNITED STATES BE RESTRICTED? *CONTINUED*

President Grover Cleveland vetoed the literacy clause of the immigration act of 1897. He believed that it unfairly discriminated against poor immigrants who never had the opportunity to go to school. He felt that these were the same kinds of immigrants who many Americans descended from. Here is an excerpt from Cleveland's veto message to Congress on March 2, 1897. (*Domain* means "land.")

> A radical departure from our national policy relating to immigrants is here presented. [In the past] we have welcomed all who come to us from other lands except those whose moral or physical condition or history threatened danger to our national welfare and safety. We have encouraged those coming from foreign countries to . . . join in the development of our vast domain, securing in return a share in the blessings of American citizenship. A century's stupendous growth, largely due to the assimilation and thrift of millions of sturdy and patriotic adopted citizens, attests the success of this generous and free-handed policy. . . .

Why did President Cleveland veto the immigration literacy clause? _____

_____

_____

Note: Two days after President Cleveland issued this veto, his term in office ended. Many in Congress were confident that they would quickly pass the literacy-test clause again. They also hoped that the new president, William McKinley, would sign it.

PART B Essay: Imagine that you are writing a newspaper editorial on the topic of future immigration. Should the U.S. "golden door" remain open? Or should the United States begin to restrict and limit future immigration by allowing entry only to those who are educated?

DBQ 13: HOW DID THE PROGRESSIVES ATTACK CHILD LABOR?

Historical Background

Children have always worked in the United States. In fact, until the past century or so, their work was their schooling. Years ago boys worked every day with their fathers. This taught them skills that would provide their livelihoods when they grew to adulthood. Most often their fathers were farmers, or fishermen, or skilled tradesmen. Boys knew that they would probably grow up to work at the same job. Working alongside their fathers was preparation for life. In the same way, girls worked with their mothers. They learned to cook, sew, and care for younger siblings, preparing for what would be their life's work. In those earlier times, before industrialism, this kind of child labor was generally good and wholesome. Children were learning as they worked. In most cases their bosses—Mom and Dad—loved them, watched out for them, and made sure that they were safe.

This all changed with the coming of industrialism. Poor peasant immigrants from Europe swarmed into cities and mining and mill towns searching for work. American farm families whose farms had failed joined them. They all became wage workers. Their lives were now controlled by assembly lines, conveyor belts, whistles, and bells. They found themselves doing very dangerous work, often with hazardous machinery and in unsafe workplaces. Poverty forced fathers, mothers, and children to take these jobs. Now, in this new industrial age, child labor took on a wholly different look. No longer was it healthful and wholesome. No longer was it schooling for future adult careers. No longer was it supervised by Mom and Dad. Now work was drudgery and dangerous. Sometimes it was even deadly.

The plight of working children in this new industrial age frightened the social reformers of the Progressive Era. The census of 1900 reported that almost two million children between the ages of ten and fifteen were employed. This totaled almost 20 percent of all children of that age bracket. Hundreds of thousands of even younger working children weren't reported in the data. Reformers were outraged. It seemed a tragedy, both for the children and for society as a whole. So many young lives were being wasted. So many children were being deprived of the schooling they needed in order to break out of poverty.

The Progressive reformers launched a battle against child labor on many fronts. Social workers like Jane Addams and Florence Kelley established settlement houses in the city slums. These neighborhood centers provided direct aid and advice to poor families. Educators such as John Dewey and G. Stanley Hall created school programs designed to prepare poor children for better lives. They also encouraged states to pass laws requiring students to attend school. Labor leaders and political leaders worked for passage of child labor laws. These laws would limit the kinds of work children could do. They would also limit the ages of employment and the numbers of hours that children could work.

(continued)

DBQ 13: HOW DID THE PROGRESSIVES ATTACK CHILD LABOR? *CONTINUED*

But in many ways, the most important battle against child labor was led by the muckraking journalists. These writers focused on exposing social problems. Their books, articles, speeches, and photographs brought the issue of child labor to the public's attention. The muckrakers knew that little change would occur unless the educated and well-off middle class could be awakened to the plight of child laborers. Somehow the wellborn and comfortable classes had to be shocked into action. They were the people whose own children were clean and well dressed, and went to school and summer camp. They were the people who had economic and political influence. Unless their conscience could be pricked and their sense of decency and fair play aroused, nothing would happen. Some of the muckraking journalists set out to do this. They focused on making the public aware of child labor and rousing the public to demand an end to it.

■ **Directions:** The following question is based on the documents (1–6) that follow. Before reading these documents, be sure to

1. Carefully read and think about the document-based question that follows these directions.

2. Ask yourself: What do I already know about this question and its topic? What did I learn from reading the Historical Background section? If I had to answer the document-based question without reading any of the documents, what would I say?

3. Take a few minutes to jot down the major things you already know about this topic and question. What important names, dates, events, and major ideas do you already know?

4. Now, read each document carefully. Ask yourself: How does this document help to answer the document-based question? Underline things of special importance and jot notes in the margins. If you're confused by or don't understand a document, go on to the next one. Later, if you have time, you can go back.

5. Develop a thesis statement that directly answers the document-based question. You'll want to state this thesis early in your essay.

6. Briefly outline your entire essay. Make sure that what you say in it supports and proves your thesis statement. In your essay, plan how you'll use the information found in the documents and what you know already about this topic.

7. Carefully write your essay. As you include supportive information from documents, be sure to cite the sources of this information. This will add authority and credibility to what you're saying.

(continued)

DBQ 13: HOW DID THE PROGRESSIVES ATTACK CHILD LABOR? *CONTINUED*

> **Question: What arguments and types of appeals did the Progressive muckrakers use to arouse the conscience of the American public to put an end to the wrongs of child labor?**

PART A   The following documents will help you to answer the document-based question. Read each document carefully. Answer the question or questions that follow each document.

Document 1

John Spargo's best-selling book *The Bitter Cry of the Children* was published in 1906. It was a milestone in the effort to awaken the American public to the realities of child labor. When it was first published, book reviews were glowing in their praise. One article noted the book's "direct and cogent appeal to the home feeling, the national interest, and the social conscience." Another called it "a painfully interesting study." *Arena* magazine devoted seven pages to its review of the book and encouraged "all persons who love justice and human rights" to read it. Though the book was mainly narrative, it did include some harsh photos of laboring children and some charts and graphs. The following charts come from Chapter 2 of the book. (Note that on the chart the term "artisan class" marks the children of the working class. The term "non-laboring class" means the wealthier, middle class.)

The School Child				
Average Height in Inches				
Age	**13**	**14**	**15**	**16**
Non-Laboring class	58.79	61.11	63.47	66.40
Artisan class	55.93	57.76	60.58	62.93
Difference	2.66	3.35	2.89	3.47

(continued)

DBQ 13: HOW DID THE PROGRESSIVES ATTACK CHILD LABOR? *CONTINUED*

Average Weight in Pounds				
Age	13	14	15	16
Non-Laboring class	88.60	99.21	110.42	128.34
Artisan class	78.27	84.61	96.79	108.70
Difference	10.33	14.60	13.63	19.64
Average Chest Girth in Inches				
Age	13	14	15	16
Non-Laboring class	28.41	29.65	30.72	33.08
Artisan class	25.24	26.28	27.51	28.97
Difference	3.17	3.37	3.21	4.11

Source: John Spargo, *The Bitter Cry of the Children,* 1906.

Summarize the general message of these three charts. _____

_____

_____

_____

_____

Document 2

Here is another chart from John Spargo's book *The Bitter Cry of the Children.* It is from Chapter 3, "The Working Child." Spargo asked probation officers in six large cities to list the occupations with the highest number of juvenile delinquents—that is, young people who committed criminal or antisocial acts. He summarized their responses in a chart like the one on the next page. The numbers 1 to 6 stand for the cities where the probation officers worked.

(continued)

DBQ 13: HOW DID THE PROGRESSIVES ATTACK CHILD LABOR? *CONTINUED*

Occupations of Juvenile Deliquents in Six Large Cities, Showing the Relative Number of Each Occupation				
Cities	A	B	C	D
1	Messenger boys	Newsboys	Factory boys	Miscellaneous
2	Newsboys	Messenger boys	Factory boys	Truants
3	Newsboys	Messenger boys	Truants	Factory boys
4	Messenger boys	Factory boys	Newsboys	Miscellaneous
5	Messenger boys	Newsboys	Truants	Miscellaneous
6	Factory boys	Truants	Messenger boys	Newsboys

Source: John Spargo, *The Bitter Cry of the Children*, 1906.

In this chart, Spargo was trying to show the reading public one of the costs to society of child labor. Explain. _____

_____

Document 3

Helen Campbell was one of the first authors to expose the evils of child labor. She did this in her 1893 book, *Darkness and Daylight; or, Lights and Shadows of New York Life*. Here, she talks about what was a very common but often-overlooked form of child labor. Thousands of young girls, some only six or seven years old, worked at home every day. They did household chores and cared for younger siblings while their parents were at their jobs. (*Debility* means "weakness.")

> It is astonishing to see the real motherliness of the little things, who lug about the baby with real devotion; and if they feed it on strange diet they are but following in the footsteps of the mothers, who regard the baby at six months old as the sharer of whatever the family . . . has to offer.
>
> This is one phase of child-labor, and the most natural and innocent one, though it is a heavy burden to lay on small shoulders, and premature age and debility are its inevitable results.

Source: Helen Campbell, *Darkness and Daylight; or, Lights and Shadows of New York Life*, A. D. Worthington & Co., 1893.

(continued)

DBQ 13: HOW DID THE PROGRESSIVES ATTACK CHILD LABOR? *CONTINUED*

Why did Helen Campbell include this story of these "little mothers" in her book? What message was she trying to send to the reading public? _____

_____

_____

_____

Document 4

John Spargo did a great deal of research for his book *The Bitter Cry of the Children*. He traveled all through the United States visiting various places where children worked. One of those places was a coal mine near Pittston, Pennsylvania. There, he watched a dozen children working as "breaker boys." Breaker boys sat on benches, crouched over coal chutes. As coal slurry rushed below them, they quickly picked out pieces of slate and other refuse. Breaker boys typically did this kind of work for ten hours each day. Spargo tried to do the job himself, but after fifteen minutes he gave up, with cut and bruised hands, and coughing from the dust.

Here's how Spargo described his visit with the boys. (Robert Owen was an English social reformer who lived in the early nineteenth century.)

> I could not do that work and live, but there were boys of ten and twelve years of age doing it for fifty and sixty cents a day. Some of them had never seen the inside of a school; few of them could read a child's primer.
>
> As I stood in that breaker I thought of the reply of the small boy to Robert Owen. Visiting an English coal mine one day, Owen asked a twelve-year old lad if he knew God. The boy stared vacantly at his questioner: "God?" he said, "God? No, I don't. He must work in some other mine." It was hard to realize amid the danger and din and blackness of that Pennsylvania breaker that such a thing as belief in a great All-good God existed.

Source: John Spargo, *The Bitter Cry of the Children*, 1906.

Analyze Spargo's description of the breaker boys. What things in this description do you suppose were especially upsetting to the readers of 1906? _____

_____

_____

_____

(continued)

DBQ 13: HOW DID THE PROGRESSIVES ATTACK CHILD LABOR? CONTINUED

Document 5

Here is another excerpt from Spargo's *The Bitter Cry of the Children.*

> The moral ills resulting from child labor are numerous and far-reaching. When children become wage-earners and are thrown into constant association with adult workers, they develop prematurely an adult consciousness and view of life . . . the first consequence of their employment is that they cease almost at once to be children. They lose their respect for parental authority, in many cases, and become arrogant, wayward, and defiant. . . . No writer dare write, and no publisher dare publish, a truthful description of the moral atmosphere of hundreds of places where children are employed. . . .

Source: John Spargo, *The Bitter Cry of the Children*, 1906.

How was Spargo trying, in this description, to turn his readers against child labor?

_____

_____

Document 6

Here is another excerpt from Spargo's book.

> We are to-day using up the vitality of children; soon they will be men and women, without the vitality and strength necessary to maintain themselves and their dependents. When we exploit the immature strength of little children, we prepare [them] for . . . the unfit and unemployable, whose lot is a shameful and debasing poverty.

Source: John Spargo, *The Bitter Cry of the Children*, 1906.

How was Spargo trying, in this description, to turn his readers against child labor?

_____

_____

PART B Essay: What arguments and types of appeals did the Progressive muckrakers use to arouse the conscience of the American public to put an end to the wrongs of child labor?

89   *Document-Based Assessment for U.S. History*

DBQ 14: THE GREAT WAR IN EUROPE: WERE WE RIGHT TO FIGHT?

Historical Background

In August 1914, World War I began. Almost all of Europe was quickly involved. Most Americans, though alarmed, generally felt safe in the United States. After all, 3,000 miles of Atlantic Ocean separated our nation from Europe's war. Many Americans also felt a little smug. Europeans may have lost their senses, madly rushing into what would be the most violent and costly war in history, but not Americans! Only days after war broke out, President Woodrow Wilson spoke for the nation. "The United States," he said, "must be neutral in fact as well as in name . . . impartial in thought as well as in action." Americans hoped that their nation would be able to stay out of Europe's awful war.

But this wasn't possible. Less than three years later, in April 1917, the United States entered World War I. It joined the side of England, France, and Russia. U.S. efforts to remain neutral had failed. Americans, too, were now caught up in the horrors of a world war.

When it was all over, in the autumn of 1918, the horrendous costs of the war were tallied up. Tanks, submarines, airplanes, machine guns, and trench warfare had created an awful toll of dead and wounded. The dead totaled almost 2,000,000 Germans, 1,700,000 Russians, 1,400,000 Frenchmen, 900,000 Britons, and 112,000 Americans. Twice as many had been wounded, and many of these were maimed and crippled for life. Almost all of the dead and wounded were young men, many of them only teenagers. Today, almost every European town and city, and many in the United States, have monuments remembering the "Great War." Most of these monuments list the names of the local men who were killed. World War I was a dreadful cost to those communities, and to millions of mothers, fathers, brothers, sisters, wives, and children.

People in all nations like to believe that wars are worth the costs. Citizens prefer to think that young men are sent to death in battle for good causes. Maybe this wasn't true of World War I. Maybe the costs were simply too high and the gains of the war too meager. After all, the peace of 1918 failed to last. Only twenty-one years later a world war broke out again. Sadly, the costs of World War II were much greater.

Maybe the United States should have simply stayed out of World War I.

■ **Directions:** The following question is based on the documents (1–6) that follow. Before reading these documents, be sure to

1. Carefully read and think about the document-based question that follows these directions.

2. Ask yourself: What do I already know about this question and its topic? What did I learn from reading the Historical Background section? If I had to answer the document-based question without reading any of the documents, what would I say?

(continued)

DBQ 14: THE GREAT WAR IN EUROPE: WERE WE RIGHT TO FIGHT? *CONTINUED*

3. Take a few minutes to jot down the major things you already know about this topic and question. What important names, dates, events, and major ideas do you already know?

4. Now read each document carefully. Ask yourself: How does this document help to answer the document-based question? Underline things of special importance and jot notes in the margins. If you're confused by, or don't understand a document, go on to the next one. Later, if you have time, you can go back.

5. Develop a thesis statement that directly answers the document-based question. You'll want to state this thesis early in your essay.

6. Briefly outline your entire essay. Make sure that what you say in it supports and proves your thesis statement. In your essay, plan how you'll use the information found in the documents and what you know already about this topic.

7. Carefully write your essay. As you include supportive information from documents, be sure to cite the sources of this information. This will add authority and credibility to what you're saying.

Question: In April 1917, the United States entered World War I on the side of England, France, and Russia. Was this the correct decision?

PART A The following documents will help you to answer the document-based question. Read each document carefully. Answer the question or questions that follow each document.

Document 1

On April 2, 1917, as President Woodrow Wilson stood before Congress, he asked Congress to declare war on Germany. He began by telling Congress about this:

> . . the extraordinary announcement of the Imperial German Government that . . . it [has] put aside all restraints of law . . . [to] use its submarines to sink every vessel that sought to approach . . . the ports of Great Britain. . . .

This announcement by Germany meant that German submarines would attack and sink any U.S. ships that attempted to deliver goods to Britain. Wilson referred to this in the speech as a "war against all nations."

(continued)

DBQ 14: THE GREAT WAR IN EUROPE: WERE WE RIGHT TO FIGHT? *CONTINUED*

Wilson continued in his speech:

> I advise that the Congress declare the recent course of the Imperial German Government to be in fact nothing less than war against the Government and people of the United States. . . .

Why did President Wilson believe that Germany's actions justified U.S. entrance into the war on the side of England, France, and Russia? _____

_____

_____

Document 2

Senator George Norris was a Republican from Nebraska. He was one of the fifty-six members of Congress who voted against Wilson's request for a declaration of war. He made a speech in Congress about his position on April 6, 1917. He began his speech by declaring, "I am most emphatically and sincerely opposed to taking any step that will force our country into the useless and senseless war now being waged in Europe." He went on to explain how President Wilson had violated his 1914 pledge of keeping the United States neutral. Norris pointed out how Wilson had encouraged wartime trade with England and France. He noted that Wilson had allowed U.S. banks and businesses to loan millions of dollars to both countries. Norris then said:

> . . . we ought to have maintained from the beginning . . . the strictest neutrality. If we had done this I do not believe we would [be] on the verge of war at the present time.
>
> To whom does war bring prosperity? . . . to the stock gambler on Wall Street—to those who are already in possession of more wealth than can be realized or enjoyed.
>
> Their object in having war . . . is to make money. Human suffering and the sacrifice of human life are necessary, but Wall Street considers only dollars and cents.
>
> We are taking a step today that is fraught with untold danger. We are going into war upon the command of gold. . . .

(continued)

DBQ 14: THE GREAT WAR IN EUROPE: WERE WE RIGHT TO FIGHT? *CONTINUED*

Why did Senator Norris oppose U.S. entrance into World War I? _____

_____

_____

Document 3

Senator Robert La Follette was a Republican from Wisconsin. He also opposed Wilson's request for a declaration of war. Here, in a speech he gave on April 6, 1917, he explained why.

> . . . I have received some 15,000 letters and telegrams . . . 9 out of 10 are an unqualified endorsement of my . . . opposing war with Germany. . . .
>
> Do not these messages indicate on the part of the people a deep-seated conviction that the United States should not enter the European war?
>
> The poor, Sir, who are the ones called upon to rot in the trenches, have no organized power, have no press to voice their will upon this question of peace or war. . . .

Why did Senator La Follette oppose U.S. entrance into World War I? _____

_____

_____

Document 4

Years after the war, in the 1930s, Congress held a series of hearings investigating the munitions industry. (Munitions businesses produce wartime weapons and equipment.) Those investigations exposed the huge profits made by the munitions industry and other corporations during World War I. The committee's report also suggested that U.S. bankers had pressured President Wilson to support England and France in 1917. The bankers had done this, the report implied, in order to protect the millions of dollars in loans that banks had made to those countries.

This committee's report had a major impact on public opinion about U.S. entrance into World War I. Here are the results of a public opinion poll taken in April 1938 by the Gallup polling organization.

(continued)

DBQ 14: THE GREAT WAR IN EUROPE: WERE WE RIGHT TO FIGHT? *CONTINUED*

> Question: Do you think it was a mistake for the United States to enter the last war (World War I)?
>
> **Yes**   **No**   **Undecided**
> 64%   28%   8%

How did most Americans in 1937 remember their country's involvement in World War I? _____

_____

Document 5

Many people, both in 1917 and in the years since, supported Wilson's decision to go to war. They pointed to the long list of crimes and atrocities that Germany committed during the period of U.S. neutrality. Surely these actions justified or even required the United States to declare war, supporters of Wilson's decision believed. Here is a list of some of Germany's actions.

> **August 1914** Germany brutally invaded and conquered Belgium, a small neutral nation. This was a gross violation of international law.
>
> **May 1915** A German submarine torpedoed and sank the *Lusitania,* a British passenger ship. Almost 1,200 civilians were killed, including 128 Americans.
>
> **January 1917** Germany announced that it was beginning unrestricted submarine warfare. This meant that Germany would attack any ships attempting to bring goods to England or France. Within weeks German submarines began sinking U.S. merchant vessels, killing American citizens.
>
> **February 1917** U.S. newspapers published a telegram from the German government to the Mexican government. Germany offered an alliance with Mexico if the United States and Germany went to war. Upon German victory, Mexico would get back the lands that it lost to the United States in the Mexican War. (Historians refer to this incident as the Zimmerman Telegram.)

How did these incidents affect U.S. public opinion about the war in Europe?

_____

_____

(continued)

DBQ 14: THE GREAT WAR IN EUROPE: WERE WE RIGHT TO FIGHT? *CONTINUED*

Document 6

The United States entered the war late. It took months to raise and train a U.S. army and then to begin sending troops to Europe. By the spring of 1918, only 300,000 U.S. troops had arrived. But historians believe that these and the other U.S. troops that arrived in the following months were just enough to turn the tide. With the help of these U.S. troops, the Allies were able first to stop and then to reverse the German attack on the Western Front. Germany's offensive in May and June of 1918 pushed the German lines to within forty-five miles of the city of Paris. Then, on July 15, the Germans tried one final push. But at Soissons, the Germans met U.S. units. The Germans were stopped here. General Pershing, the U.S. commander in Europe, said this "turned the tide of the war." Even the Germans now knew that the war was over. The German chancellor wrote this:

> On the 18th [of July] even the most optimistic among us knew that all was lost. The history of the world was played out in three days.

Without the help of the Americans, it seems likely that Germany would have won the war. It would have defeated England and France.

Does this justify U.S. involvement in World War I, knowing that without it, Germany likely would have won? Why or why not? _____

_____

_____

 PART B Essay: In April 1917, the United States entered World War I on the side of England, France, and Russia. Was this the correct decision?

DBQ 15: WHAT CAUSED THE GREAT DEPRESSION?

Historical Background

Today, the Great Depression of the 1930s is only a distant childhood memory for our country's oldest citizens. For many, it's a sad memory. Some remember seeing worry and fear in their parents' eyes. Others remember losing the family home or farm and having to move in with relatives. Many recall seeing long lines of people at soup kitchens, or groups of unemployed men hanging around on street corners. Some look back painfully to times of actual hunger and suffering. Even today, more than six decades later, some are still angry and bitter as they remember the Great Depression years of the 1930s.

Behind their personal memories are cold, hard facts. Between 1930 and 1933 in the United States the following happened:

- 12 million workers lost their jobs. One in four of all workers became unemployed.

- 85,000 businesses went bankrupt.

- 8,000 banks closed. Millions of families lost their life savings.

- 500,000 farm mortgages were foreclosed. Farm families either became renters or were forced off the land.

- Total national income dropped by almost 50 percent.

Never before or since have Americans suffered such a long and terrible economic crisis as the Great Depression of the 1930s.

What caused the Great Depression? Economists and historians have argued and debated its origins. But almost all agree about one fundamental cause—overproduction. In 1929, the United States simply had too many products and not enough consumers with money to purchase them. The stock market crashed in late 1929. A chain of events quickly followed, and the country sank into economic ruin. People stopped spending money. Unsold goods backed up in warehouses. Factories and businesses reduced production. Workers were laid off, and families lost their incomes. People stopped spending money. . . .

All of this is sadly understandable. But the bigger question remains. Why, by the end of the 1920s, was the U.S. economy producing more goods than it could sell? The following documents provide some clues.

■ **Directions:** The following question is based on the documents (1–4) that follow. Before reading these documents, be sure to

    1. Carefully read and think about the document-based question that follows these directions. *(continued)*

DBQ 15: WHAT CAUSED THE GREAT DEPRESSION? *CONTINUED*

2. Ask yourself: What do I already know about this question and its topic? What did I learn from reading the Historical Background section? If I had to answer the document-based question without reading any of the documents, what would I say?

3. Take a few minutes to jot down the major things you already know about this topic and question. What important names, dates, events, and major ideas do you already know?

4. Now read each document carefully. Ask yourself: How does this document help to answer the document-based question? Underline things of special importance and jot notes in the margins. If you're confused by or don't understand a document, go on to the next one. Later, if you have time, you can go back.

5. Develop a thesis statement that directly answers the document-based question. You'll want to state this thesis early in your essay.

6. Briefly outline your entire essay. Make sure that what you say in it supports and proves your thesis statement. In your essay, plan how you'll use the information found in the documents and what you know already about this topic.

7. Carefully write your essay. As you include supportive information from documents, be sure to cite the sources of this information. This will add authority and credibility to what you're saying.

Question: What caused the Great Depression?

The following documents will help you answer the document-based question. Read each document carefully. Answer the question or questions that follow each document.

Document 1

A stock exchange is the market where stocks in companies are bought and sold. Just as at an auction, the price of each company's stock is determined by demand—by how much people want the stock. If people think that the company is a good one and that the value of the stock will go up, they will purchase shares. This will move the price of shares higher. On the other hand, if people think that the value of the company and its stock will fall, owners of the stock will probably want to sell. This will move share prices lower. It's this ongoing buying and selling of millions of shares of stock that moves the prices of stocks up and down each day.

(continued)

DBQ 15: WHAT CAUSED THE GREAT DEPRESSION? *CONTINUED*

During the 1920s, the prices of stock bought and sold on the New York Stock Exchange skyrocketed. In the year 1924, the average price was $104. (These average prices are from the Dow Jones Industrial Average.) People were confident that the U.S. economy was growing and that stock prices were going to rise. Believing this, buyers bid up the prices of stock. By 1929, the average price had risen to $290. On September 3, 1929, the average stock price reached $381.17. But then, in just a matter of days, stock prices began to plummet. In the following eight weeks, General Electric Company's stock prices fell from almost $400 to only $168 per share. A share of stock in Montgomery Ward fell from $137 to $49. During just those two months, investors lost $40 billion in stock value. Worse, stock prices continued to tumble. By 1933, four years later, stocks had lost 75 percent of their value. Montgomery Ward stock had fallen to $4 per share. Millions of Americans were wiped out, losing all that they owned.

The Dow Jones Industrial Average shows the average price of a number of stocks traded on the New York Stock Exchange. The chart below shows the value of the stocks tracked by the Dow Jones Industrial Average between 1920 and 1930.

(continued)

DBQ 15: WHAT CAUSED THE GREAT DEPRESSION? *CONTINUED*

Many Americans lost their life savings when the stock market crashed. How do you suppose this affected their spending habits? _____

How did this affect the total amount of consumer demand? _____

_____

Document 2

Today, less than 2 percent of the U.S. workforce works in agriculture. But in the 1920s, over 20 percent—one person in every five workers—worked on farms. A great number of people depended on agriculture for their livelihood. So the prices of farm goods and the earnings of farms had huge impacts on the entire economy.

During World War I (1914–1918), U.S. farm income was high. U.S. farmers were selling millions of dollars worth of corn, wheat, beef, and other farm products to Europe. Between 1914 and 1918, U.S. annual farm income increased from $4 billion to $10 billion. During these good times, U.S. farmers borrowed money to purchase machinery and expand production. But with peace and the end of the war, Europe's demand for American farm goods fell. Agricultural prices dropped. So, too, did the incomes of U.S. farmers. Many farmers now found themselves with high debts and little income. This chart shows how farm prices (and therefore farmers' incomes) changed from the wartime prices of 1918 through the 1920s.

U.S. Farm Prices, 1918–1928				
	Corn $/bushel	Wheat $/bushel	Beef (index)	Hogs (index)
1918	1.52	2.08	50	19
1920	.64	1.53	39	20
1922	.73	.97	30	10
1924	1.05	.83	21	10
1926	.74	1.20	34	12
1928	.84	1.00	50	13

(continued)

DBQ 15: WHAT CAUSED THE GREAT DEPRESSION? *CONTINUED*

What happened to American farm prices after the war ended? _____

_____

_____

What impact did this have on the ability of farm families to purchase consumer goods during the 1920s? _____

_____

_____

Document 3

The 1920s saw major growth in industrial production of consumer products. Factory assembly lines turned out automobiles, refrigerators, electric stoves, and radios as fast as consumers could buy them. To keep consumer demand high, business developed a new financial practice. Businesses sold their goods on credit. They allowed consumers to purchase products with small payments over a long period of time. Families sometimes didn't have enough money to pay for something they wanted right then. They could still get it by buying it on credit. But there were dangers in having large numbers of families deeply in debt. Here's how one historian described the problem.

> . . . the purchasing power of workers and farmers was not great enough to sustain prosperity. For a time this was partly [solved] by the fact that consumers bought goods on installment at a rate faster than their income was expanding, but it was inevitable that a time would come when they would have to reduce purchases, and the cutback in buying would sap the whole economy.

Source: William E. Leuchtenburg, *The Perils of Prosperity, 1914–32,* University of Chicago Press, 1958.

Buying on credit allowed families, for a time, to spend more money than they had. But the time came when families were so deeply in debt that they had to stop spending. How did this affect the economy? _____

_____

_____

(continued)

DBQ 15: WHAT CAUSED THE GREAT DEPRESSION? *CONTINUED*

Document 4

During the 1920s, the rich got richer, and the poor got poorer. By 1929, the richest 30,000 families had more wealth than the poorest 10 million families. These 10 million families made up the poorest 40 percent of the entire U.S. population at that time. The richest 30,000 families made up only about one tenth of one percent of the population. The few rich were very wealthy, while many Americans were barely getting by.

This unequal distribution of wealth made it difficult for society to purchase all of the goods that were being produced. If more wealth had been in the hands of more people, it would have resulted in greater spending and purchasing of consumer goods. But the rich families saved much of their wealth instead of spending it. Much of these savings were either invested into businesses or speculated on the stock exchange.

How did the unequal distribution of wealth during the 1920s contribute to the fundamental cause of the Great Depression? _____

_____

PART B   Essay: What caused the Great Depression?

DBQ 16: THE ELECTION OF 1936: SHOULD THE NEW DEAL CONTINUE?

Historical Background

President Franklin Delano Roosevelt (FDR) ran for reelection in 1936. His opponent was Kansas governor Alfred Landon, the nominee of the Republican Party. Roosevelt was finishing his first term in office. During those four years, he had launched a massive effort by the federal government to pull the nation out of the Great Depression. The many programs of this effort were called the New Deal. They included such things as the Public Works Administration, the Civilian Conservation Corps, the Agricultural Adjustment Act, the Tennessee Valley Authority, the Works Progress Administration, the Social Security Act, and the National Labor Relations Act. FDR and his supporters were proud of these programs. They hoped that the programs would lessen suffering and help to end the Great Depression.

Landon's supporters voiced angry opposition to Roosevelt and his New Deal programs. Two themes marked their protests. These themes were the "reckless spending" of the federal government and the "dictatorial powers" being wielded by FDR. Campaign slogans condemned Franklin "Deficit" Roosevelt and his New Deal. Instead of a "New Deal," they demanded a "New Deck." Landon's supporters were confident that the American voters would support their campaign against Roosevelt. They predicted a "Landon-slide" victory on Election Day.

Roosevelt and his supporters fought back. They claimed that the Republican Party represented the interests of the wealthy and big business. They blamed the Republican presidents of the 1920s for causing the Great Depression. Millions of the poor and unemployed agreed with these charges. FDR's campaign speeches drew huge crowds of cheering supporters. As Election Day approached, FDR was confident of victory.

But the outcome of the election was uncertain. Most of the nation's newspapers supported Landon. So, too, did most of the nation's wealthy and powerful interests. The *Literary Digest* poll, which had correctly identified the winners of the last six presidential elections, was predicting a Landon victory.

■ **Directions:** The following question is based on the documents (1–4) that follow. Before reading these documents, be sure to

1. Carefully read and think about the document-based question that follows these directions.

2. Ask yourself: What do I already know about this question and its topic? What did I learn from reading the Historical Background section? If I had to answer the document-based question without reading any of the documents, what would I say?

3. Take a few minutes to jot down the major things you already know about this topic and question. What important names, dates, events, and major ideas do you already know?

(continued)

DBQ 16: THE ELECTION OF 1936: SHOULD THE NEW DEAL CONTINUE? *CONTINUED*

4. Now read each document carefully. Ask yourself: How does this document help to answer the document-based question? Underline things of special importance and jot notes in the margins. If you're confused by or don't understand a document, go on to the next one. Later, if you have time, you can go back.

5. Develop a thesis statement that directly answers the document-based question. You'll want to state this thesis early in your essay.

6. Briefly outline your entire essay. Make sure that what you say in it supports and proves your thesis statement. In your essay, plan how you'll use the information found in the documents and what you already know about this topic.

7. Carefully write your essay. As you include supportive information from documents, be sure to cite the sources of this information. This will add authority and credibility to what you're saying.

Question: It's 1936. Who should be elected president, Roosevelt or Landon?

PART A The following documents will help you answer the document-based question. Read each document carefully. Answer the question or questions that follow each document.

Document 1

Republican Party leaders met in Cleveland at the 1936 nominating convention. They chose Alfred Landon as their party's presidential nominee. They also wrote and adopted the official party platform. The platform stated the party's beliefs and goals. Here are some excerpts from the 1936 Republican Party platform. (*Usurp* means "to take something without the right to do so.")

(continued)

DBQ 16: THE ELECTION OF 1936: SHOULD THE NEW DEAL CONTINUE? *CONTINUED*

> America is in peril. The welfare of American men and women and the future of our youth are at stake.
>
> The powers of Congress have been usurped by the President. The rights and liberties of American citizens have been violated. The New Deal Administration constantly seeks to usurp the rights reserved to the States and the people.
>
> It [the New Deal] has insisted on the passage of laws contrary to the Constitution.

What common theme do these attacks on FDR and his administration express?

_____

_____

_____

Document 2

Here are additional excerpts from the 1936 Republican Party platform.

> [The New Deal Administration] has been guilty of frightful waste and extravagance. . . .
>
> It has created a vast multitude of new offices, filled them with its favorites. . . .
>
> The New Deal Administration has been characterized by shameful waste. . . .
>
> It has piled deficit upon deficit. It threatens national bankruptcy. . . .
>
> Stop the folly of uncontrolled spending. Balance the budget. . . .

What common theme does this attack on FDR and his administration express?

_____

_____

_____

(continued)

DBQ 16: THE ELECTION OF 1936: SHOULD THE NEW DEAL CONTINUE? *CONTINUED*

Document 3

As of the year 1936, how successful was FDR's New Deal in solving the problems of the Great Depression? The following charts and graphs tell part of the story. (Remember that FDR's presidency began in March 1933.)

U.S. Unemployment 1928–1936			
Year	**Event**	**Number Unemployed**	**% of Workforce Unemployed**
1928	Hoover elected	2.2 million	4.6%
1929	stock market crash	1.8 million	3.8%
1930		4.5 million	9.2%
1931		8.3 million	16.7%
1932	FDR elected	12.3 million	24.5%
1933	FDR takes office	13.1 million	25.6%
1934		11.6 million	22.4%
1935		10.9 million	20.7%
1936	FDR v. Landon election	9.3 million	17.4%

Gross National Product: The Gross National Product, or GNP, is the value of all goods and services produced during a year. In some ways, it measures the wealth of the nation.

U.S Gross National Product (GNP)	
1928	$97.5 billion
1929	$103.1 billion
1930	$90.4 billion
1931	$75.8 billion
1932	$58.0 billion
1933	$55.6 billion
1934	$65.1 billion
1935	$72.2 billion
1936	$82.5 billion

(continued)

*Document-Based Assessment for
U.S. History*

DBQ 16: THE ELECTION OF 1936: SHOULD THE NEW DEAL CONTINUE? *CONTINUED*

U.S. Federal Government Budget 1928–1936		
Year	**Total Budget**	**Total Amount Borrowed**
1928	$2.9 billion	0
1929	$3.1 billion	0
1930	$3.3 billion	0
1931	$3.6 billion	$.5 billion
1932	$4.7 billion	$2.7 billion
1933	$4.6 billion	$2.6 billion
1934	$6.6 billion	$3.6 billion
1935	$6.5 billion	$2.8 billion
1936	$8.4 billion	$4.4 billion

How successful were FDR and his New Deal policies at solving the problems of the Great Depression? Cite specific evidence from the charts to support your answer.

_____

_____

Document 4

As you would expect, former president Herbert Hoover was a fierce opponent of FDR and his New Deal programs. Here are excerpts from a speech Hoover made in support of Landon's election. Hoover delivered the speech on October 30, 1936—just a few days before Election Day.

> Through four years of experience this New Deal attack upon free institutions has emerged as the [major] issue in America.
>
> We [Landon and the Republicans] propose to turn the whole direction of this country toward liberty, not away from it [as Roosevelt has].

(continued)

DBQ 16: THE ELECTION OF 1936: SHOULD THE NEW DEAL CONTINUE? *CONTINUED*

What was Hoover accusing FDR and the New Dealers of doing? _____

_____

_____

_____

PART B

Essay: It's 1936. Who should be elected president, Roosevelt or Landon?

Imagine that it's November 2, 1936, the day before Election Day, and you're a newspaper editor. Write an editorial supporting either FDR or Landon. Do not use information or data from beyond 1936 in your essay.

DBQ 17: WHAT WERE THE COSTS AND BENEFITS OF U.S. VICTORY IN WORLD WAR II?

Historical Background

World War II was the most violent and destructive conflict in history. It began with Nazi Germany's invasion of Poland in September 1939. Warfare then spread around the globe. Eventually, more than fifty nations became involved in the fighting. For six horrible years, war was waged on a scale never before seen. When it was finally over and the costs tallied, the numbers of dead and wounded were almost unbelievable. In all, more than 60 million people had died. Of these, probably 40 million were civilians.

The greatest casualties were suffered by U.S. allies, especially the Soviet Union and China. Together, these two nations lost over 30 million people. The casualities of other Allies were small in comparison, although horrible. The French dead numbered 480,000, and the British dead numbered 368,000. The United States lost 418,000 people. Germany, Italy, and Japan had been the Axis Powers. Together they lost about 8 million soldiers and 4 million civilians. More than 100,000 of those civilian deaths were Japanese. They resulted from the atomic bombs dropped by the United States on the cities of Hiroshima and Nagasaki in the final weeks of the war.

The costs in human lives and physical destruction were undeniably awful. But few of the victors doubted the need to fight World War II. The evils of fascism became clearer and more obvious as Allied troops slowly occupied Germany and Poland in the last months of the war. There they found gruesome death camps where millions of Jews and other victims of Hitler had been killed. This only confirmed what most people knew already: It would have been a dreadful world if Hitler, Mussolini, and Tojo had not been stopped. As terrible as World War II was, it had to be fought.

At the war's end, in 1945, the United States found its power supreme in the world. U.S. military, economic, and political power were virtually unchallenged. Americans accounted for less than 5 percent of the world's total population. Yet the United States possessed most of the world's economic wealth and industrial might. Its armed forces occupied much of Europe and Asia. Most of the world's people, including our country's defeated foes and exhausted allies, looked with hope toward the United States. They turned to our nation for leadership and help as the world put down its weapons and embraced peace.

While joyful in their triumph, Americans slowly began to see that victory in 1945 had costs as well as benefits. Leadership of the world brought with it challenges as well as opportunities. It brought fears as well as hopes.

■ **Directions:** The following question is based on the documents (1–5) that follow. Before reading these documents, be sure to

   1 . Carefully read and think about the document-based question that follows these directions.

(continued)

DBQ 17: WHAT WERE THE COSTS AND BENEFITS OF U.S. VICTORY IN WORLD WAR II? *CONTINUED*

2. Ask yourself: What do I already know about this question and its topic? What did I learn from reading the Historical Background section? If I had to answer the document-based question without reading any of the documents, what would I say?

3. Take a few minutes to jot down the major things you already know about this topic and question. What important names, dates, events, and major ideas do you already know?

4. Now read each document carefully. Ask yourself: How does this document help to answer the document-based question? Underline things of special importance and jot notes in the margins. If you're confused by or don't understand a document, go on to the next one. Later, if you have time, you can go back.

5. Develop a thesis statement that directly answers the document-based question. You'll want to state this thesis early in your essay.

6. Briefly outline your entire essay. Make sure that what you say in it supports and proves your thesis statement. In your essay, plan how you'll use the information found in the documents and what you know already about this topic.

7. Carefully write your essay. As you include supportive information from documents, be sure to cite the sources of this information. This will add authority and credibility to what you're saying.

> **Question: What costs and challenges, and what benefits and opportunities, came with U.S. victory in World War II?**

PART A The following documents will help you answer the document-based question. Read each document carefully. Answer the question or questions that follow each document.

Document 1

It's difficult to measure the true financial costs to Americans of World War II. But one way to try is to look at how much the national government spent during each year of the war. Then see how much of this spending went directly for military expenditures. As you study these costs, remember that American taxpayers paid for them. Taxpayers paid some of these costs directly through higher taxes during the war years. Taxpayers paid some other costs years later, over time. These payments covered the billions that the government had borrowed in the form of war bonds.

(continued)

DBQ 17: WHAT WERE THE COSTS AND BENEFITS OF U.S. VICTORY IN WORLD WAR II? *CONTINUED*

U.S. Federal Government Spending 1938–1947		
	Total Federal Government Spending	**National Defense Costs**
1938 (prewar)	$6.8 billion	$1.1 billion
1942 (early in the war)	$34.5 billion	$23.9 billion
1945 (last year of the war)	$95.2 billion	$85.6 billion
1947 (postwar)	$36.9 billion	$13.6 billion

How much more was the federal government spending annually on war costs (national defense) in 1945 than it had only seven years earlier in 1938? _____

Document 2

Another way to measure the cost of war is in grim casualty figures. Some of these awful numbers were mentioned in the Historical Background section on page 108. This document examines these numbers in greater detail.

Deaths in World War II by Selected Countries		
	Military Deaths	**Civilian Deaths**
China	4,000,000	6,000,000
France	210,000	270,000
Germany	5,500,000	1,800,000
Great Britain	307,000	61,700
Italy	306,400	153,000
Japan	1,900,000	700,000
Soviet Union	10,600,000	11,500,000
United States	407,000	11,200

(continued)

DBQ 17: WHAT WERE THE COSTS AND BENEFITS OF U.S. VICTORY IN WORLD WAR II? *CONTINUED*

How did U.S. civilian deaths compare with civilian deaths in the other major countries involved in World War II? _____

Why were U.S. civilian casualties so much lower than those suffered by other nations?

_____

_____

Document 3

The United States emerged from World War II with the only powerful economy in the world. Unlike most other nations involved in the war, the United States had been virtually untouched by fighting. Its cities were not in ruins. Its factories and farms had not been destroyed. In fact, U.S. farms and factories were booming in 1945. Here's how one American writer described the U.S. economic situation at that time. (*Complacency* means "smugness and overconfidence.")

> Lucky for us, we were the only economy standing after World War II, and we had no serious competition for forty years. That gave us a huge head of steam but also a huge sense of entitlement and complacency. . . .

Source: Thomas Friedman, *The World Is Flat: A Brief History of the Twenty-First Century*, Farrar, Straus and Giroux, 2005, p. 252.

What effect do you suppose U.S. economic supremacy in 1945 had on the lives and lifestyles of the American public in the decades following World War II? _____

_____

_____

Document 4

The Soviet Union was the major ally of the United States in the war against Hitler's Germany. The Soviet Union was a communist country ruled by a cruel dictator. But both the United States and the Soviet Union were firmly opposed to German aggression. This mutual policy had brought these two very different nations together as allies in the war. But once Germany was defeated, the U.S. need for unity with the Soviet Union was gone. The U.S. distrust of and opposition to communism reemerged. The two countries began a face-off that soon came to be called the Cold War. The fact that the Soviets failed to withdraw their troops from Eastern Europe after the war's

(continued)

         Document-Based Assessment for U.S. History

DBQ 17: WHAT WERE THE COSTS AND BENEFITS OF U.S. VICTORY IN WORLD WAR II? *CONTINUED*

ending only added to U.S. distrust and fear. It's ironic that out of the U.S. victory over Germany came a new rivalry and new international tensions. U.S. fear of the Soviets and their fear of the United States sparked a major arms race. Each nation built new and more dangerous weapons. Here's how one historian described the birth of the Cold War between the United States and the Soviet Union. (*Red* in the excerpt refers to the Soviets.)

> . . . and when the end [of the war] came the Red army was in sole possession of . . . East Europe. This crucial result of World War II destroyed the Grand Alliance [of the United States and the Soviet Union] and gave birth to the Cold War. The West, with the United States leading the way, was unwilling to accept Russian domination of East Europe.

Source: Stephen E. Ambrose, *Rise to Globalism: American Foreign Policy, 1938–1980,* 1980, p. 93.

Irony is a word that means "contrary, inconsistent, or paradoxical." How was it ironic that the American victory in World War II resulted in new international tensions and fears for the United States? _____

_____

_____

Document 5

In 1945, the United States was not just the supreme economic power in the world. The United States was also the supreme military power. Its World War II enemies — Germany, Italy, and Japan — were defeated. Their military power was destroyed. The wartime U.S. allies, Great Britain and France, were exhausted. Even though the Soviets ended the war with a huge army occupying Eastern Europe, U.S. military might was clearly superior. Here's how Stephen Ambrose, the historian quoted in Document 4, described the military situation in 1945.

(continued)

DBQ 17: WHAT WERE THE COSTS AND BENEFITS OF U.S. VICTORY IN WORLD WAR II? *CONTINUED*

> At the conclusion of World War II America was at the top of the mountain. In all the world only the United States had a healthy economy, an intact physical plant capable of mass production of goods, and excess capital. American troops occupied Japan . . . while American influence was dominant [in much of the world]. . . . Above all, the United States had . . . the atomic bomb.

Source: Stephen E. Ambrose, *Rise to Globalism: American Foreign Policy, 1938–1980,* 1980, p. 17.

Was possession of the atomic bomb a cost and challenge, or a benefit and opportunity, for the United States in 1945? Explain. _____

_____

_____

_____

PART B Essay: What costs and challenges, and what benefits and opportunities, came with U.S. victory in World War II?

DBQ 18: HOW DID THE UNITED STATES CHANGE IN THE POSTWAR YEARS?

Historical Background

Over ten million men and women were released from U.S. military service during the twenty months following the end of World War II. They went home to take up their civilian lives where they had left off, before the war. It soon became obvious to them—and to all Americans—that the postwar years were very different from the prewar years. Before the war, Americans had been struggling with economic depression—with the Dust Bowl, unemployment, and widespread poverty. Now, only a few years later, U.S. soldiers returned to a prosperous society, to hopes and plans for the future. This same prosperity and optimism marked the following twenty years, through the 1940s, the 1950s, and into the 1960s. During these years, massive social changes transformed the lives of Americans throughout the nation. For most Americans, life in the year 1960 was astonishingly different from what it had been like only twenty-five years earlier, in 1935. It was much more prosperous and, for most, much happier.

■ **Directions:** The following question is based on the documents (1–6) that follow. Before reading these documents, be sure to

1. Carefully read and think about the document-based question that follows these directions.

2. Ask yourself: What do I already know about this question and its topic? What did I learn from reading the Historical Background section? If I had to answer the document-based question without reading any of the documents, what would I say?

3. Take a few minutes to jot down the major things you already know about this topic and question. What important dates, events, and major ideas do you already know?

4. Now read each document carefully. Ask yourself: How does this document help to answer the document-based question? Underline things of special importance and jot notes in the margins. If you're confused by or don't understand a document, go on to the next one. Later, if you have time, you can go back.

5. Develop a thesis statement that directly answers the document-based question. You'll want to state this thesis early in your essay.

6. Briefly outline your entire essay. Make sure that what you say in it supports and proves your thesis statement. In your essay, plan how you'll use the information found in the documents and what you know already about this topic.

7. Carefully write your essay. As you include supportive information from documents, be sure to cite the sources of this information. This will add authority and credibility to what you're saying.

(continued)

DBQ 18: HOW DID THE UNITED STATES CHANGE IN THE POSTWAR YEARS? *CONTINUED*

Question: How was U.S. society in the post–World War II decades different from U.S. society of the prewar decades?

PART A The following documents will help you answer the document-based question. Read each document carefully. Answer the question or questions that follow each document.

Document 1

Demography is the study of social or population data—such things as births, deaths, marriage and divorce rates, migration, and immigration. The following charts and tables show some of the demographic changes in the United States in the post–World War II decades.

U.S. Marriages and Births, 1935–1960				
	Number of Marriages	**Marriage Rate***	**Number of Births**	**Birthrate****
1935	1.3 million	10.2	2.3 million	77
1945	1.6 million	11.4	2.8 million	86
1946	2.3 million	16.3	3.4 million	102
1950	1.6 million	11.1	3.6 million	106
1955	1.5 million	9.1	4.1 million	119
1960	1.5 million	8.5	4.3 million	118

(* per 1,000 population; ** per 1,000 adult females)

What general statements can you make about U.S. demographics in the fifteen years following World War II? _____

_____

_____

(continued)

DBQ 18: HOW DID THE UNITED STATES CHANGE IN THE POSTWAR YEARS? *CONTINUED*

Document 2

Consumer goods are manufactured products that people and families purchase for personal use. Consumer goods that Americans purchased in the years following World War II included such things as automobiles, refrigerators, televisions, and radios. Ownership of these kinds of consumer goods greatly changed the way that people and families lived. Study the following table. As you do, think about how owning these

U.S. Consumer Goods Owned 1935–1960			
	Autos Owned	**Households with Radios**	**Televisions**
1935	22 million	10 million	0
1945	26 million	33 million	0
1950	40 million	41 million	8 million
1955	52 million	46 million	30 million
1960	62 million	50 million	46 million

consumer goods changed the lives of Americans during those years.

Considering only the table shown above, how did American life change in the fifteen years following World War II? _____

_____

_____

_____

(continued)

DBQ 18: HOW DID THE UNITED STATES CHANGE IN THE POSTWAR YEARS? CONTINUED

Document 3

The patterns of where Americans lived changed in the post–World War II decades. Study this chart to see these changes in pattern.

U.S. Residents, 1920–1960

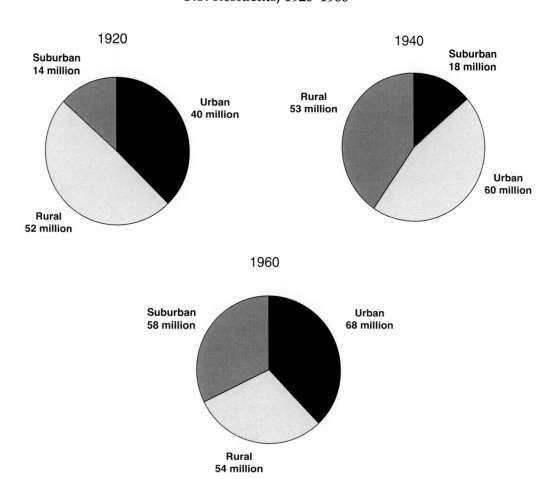

How did American living patterns change in the two decades following World War II?

_____

_____

How do you suppose suburban growth was related to the growth in the number of automobiles (see Document 1)? _____

_____

(continued)

DBQ 18: HOW DID THE UNITED STATES CHANGE IN THE POSTWAR YEARS? *CONTINUED*

Document 4

When World War II ended, many economists and government leaders feared that the United States would slip back into a depression. This would mean a return to the economic crisis that had existed before the war. Happily for Americans, just the opposite occurred. Here are some data that tell this story.

U.S per Capital Income*, 1935–1960		
Year	In Current Dollars	In 2000 Dollars**
1935	$ 474	$ 5,960
1945	$1,223	$11,700
1950	$1,501	$10,800
1955	$1,881	$12,150
1960	$ 2,219	$12,800

* Per capita income = all personal income earned in a single year, divided by the total national population.

** This figure converts each year's money amount into its value in the year 2000.

How did the income (and therefore living standards) of Americans change following World War II? _____

_____

Document 5

The decades from 1940 through 1960 saw a great change in the number of American farmers. The following chart shows this change.

U.S. Farming, 1940–1960		
	Number of U.S. Farmers	% of Total U.S. Workforce in Farming
1940	9.5 million	17%
1950	7.1 million	11%
1960	5.4 million	7%

(continued)

DBQ 18: HOW DID THE UNITED STATES CHANGE IN THE POSTWAR YEARS? *CONTINUED*

Many years ago, most Americans earned their livings as farmers. Today, less than three percent of the U.S. workforce is employed in farming. How did farm employment change in the years following World War II?

_____

_____

Document 6

During World War II, millions of young American men were serving overseas in the armed forces. Many women took jobs outside the home in order to keep the American economy running. What happened to these women after the war ended? The following chart provides some answer to this question.

U.S Adult Women Working Outside the Home, 1940–1947		
	Number	**% of Adult Women (ages 16–65)**
1940	12.1 million	27%
1941	14.6 million	32%
1942	16.1 million	35%
1943	18.8 million	40%
1944	19.4 million	42%
1945	19.4 million	41%
1946	16.8 million	35%
1947	16.6 million	33%

How did the return of the men from overseas (in 1945 and 1946) affect the employment of women?_____

How does Document 1 help to explain what happened to the women after the war?

_____

_____

PART B Essay: How was U.S. society in the post–World War II decades different from U.S. society of the prewar decades?

Name _____ Date _____

DBQ 19: HOW HAS AMERICAN SOCIETY CHANGED SINCE 1980?

Historical Background

Though you may think of 1980 as long ago, many older Americans see it as "only yesterday." Most of your grandparents were middle-aged adults in 1980, well into their forties or early fifties. Your parents were probably teenagers in high school, not much older than you are today.

As the year 1980 began, Jimmy Carter was nearing the end of his presidency. Later that year he ran for reelection. But former California governor Ronald Reagan defeated him. In 1980, you could buy a new car for $7,000 and fill the gas tank for $1.20 a gallon. You could mail a letter for 15 cents.

But while the name of our country's president was different and prices were lower, in many ways 1980 wasn't too much different from today. The lives that your parents knew when they were teenagers weren't too unlike what you know today. Most people worked in factories or offices. Most purchased food at large supermarkets and clothes at stores. Most families lived in modern homes or apartments. These homes were equipped with electricity, hot water at the turn of a tap, and central heat controlled by a thermostat. Americans watched color televisions, owned cars, and listened to rock music. Children played with their friends after school, and teenagers were on high school teams and in clubs. If you were magically transported back to 1980, you wouldn't feel out of place.

But if you look more closely, you'll see the differences. You'll be surprised at what you find.

■ **Directions:** The following question is based on the documents (1–7) that follow. Before reading these documents, be sure to

1. Carefully read and think about the document-based question that follows these directions.

2. Ask yourself: What do I already know about this question and its topic? What did I learn from reading the Historical Background section? If I had to answer the document-based question without reading any of the documents, what would I say?

3. Take a few minutes to jot down the major things you already know about this topic and question. What important names, dates, events, and major ideas do you already know?

4. Now read each document carefully. Ask yourself: How does this document help to answer the document-based question? Underline things of special importance and jot notes in the margins. If you're confused by or don't understand a document, go on to the next one. Later, if you have time, you can go back.

(continued)

DBQ 19: HOW HAS AMERICAN SOCIETY CHANGED SINCE 1980? *CONTINUED*

5. Develop a thesis statement that directly answers the document-based question. You'll want to state this thesis early in your essay.

6. Briefly outline your entire essay. Make sure that what you say in it supports and proves your thesis statement. In your essay, plan how you'll use the information found in the documents and what you know already about this topic.

7. Carefully write your essay. As you include supportive information from documents, be sure to cite the sources of this information. This will add authority and credibility to what you're saying.

Question: In what important ways has American society changed since 1980?

PART A The following documents will help you answer the document-based question. Read each document carefully. Answer the question or questions that follow each document.

Document 1

Are Americans earning larger annual incomes today than they did in 1980? The following chart answers this question.

Median Annual Incomes of Households in Current and Constant (2003) Dollars 1970–2003					
	1970	**1980**	**1990**	**2000**	**2003**
Current $* Constant $**	$8,700 $41,400	$17,700 $39,500	$29,900 $42,200	$41,900 $44,800	$43,300 $43,300

Household Income is basically family income.

* Current dollars measure the income in the dollars of that year.

**Constant dollars measure the income of each year in money equal in value to 2003 dollars.

(continued)

DBQ 19: HOW HAS AMERICAN SOCIETY CHANGED SINCE 1980? *CONTINUED*

Between 1980 and 2003, what happened to the annual incomes of typical American families? Explain. _____

_____

What happened to the annual incomes of typical American families between 2000 and 2003? _____

Document 2

Here is a short description explaining how a school principal prepared a formal letter in 1980.

> I asked my secretary to step into my office to take dictation. As I composed and dictated the letter aloud to her, she wrote it out in shorthand. (Shorthand was a system of rapid writing that used symbols for words and combinations of letters.) Then she went back to her office to type up the letter on the electric typewriter. Once in a while, she made an error in her typing. She corrected any errors using what was called white-out, a white fluid that covered the errors. She then typed the corrections over the white-out. When done, my secretary brought the letter in to me for a final proofreading. I found that she had mistakenly omitted a word from a sentence. She now had to retype the entire letter. Writing a short letter and preparing it for mailing took the two of us 33 minutes.

Compare this description with how a school principal would write a similar letter today. _____

_____

_____

Document 3

Here is a list of things you're very familiar with. No teenagers had them in 1980.

Internet	digital camera	fax machine
cell phone	scanner	video games
PDA	personal computer	iPod
e-mail	CD player	DVD player

(continued)

DBQ 19: HOW HAS AMERICAN SOCIETY CHANGED SINCE 1980? *CONTINUED*

How is your life today different from the typical teenager's life in 1980 because of these products? _____

_____

_____

Document 4

One of the biggest health challenges facing our country today is the rising number of overweight people. Government health studies report that 60 percent of American adults are overweight and that 30 percent are obese.

Obesity is affecting children and teenagers, too. Study the following chart.

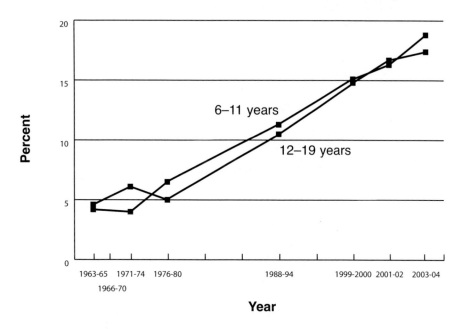

Trends in Childhood and Adolescent Obesity

Why do you suppose the number of obese children and teenagers has risen so much over the past 30 years? _____

_____

_____

(continued)

DBQ 19: HOW HAS AMERICAN SOCIETY CHANGED SINCE 1980? CONTINUED

Document 5

Fifty years ago only a small number of high school students held part-time jobs during the school year. Boys might have had paper routes, using their bikes to deliver newspapers. They might have mowed lawns on Saturdays. Many girls took babysitting jobs on Friday or Saturday nights. But working in a store or factory for twenty or more hours each week during the school year was very uncommon. Today that's all changed. Let's see how much it's changed in the past three decades, since your parents were your age.

Employment of U.S. High School Students, 1980 and 2005		
	1980	**2005**
All 12th Graders	64%	87%
All 10th Graders	44%	65%

Is employment during the school year good or bad for high school students? Why or why not? _____

_____

_____

Document 6

How frugal are Americans? Are they savers or are they spenders? Is their desire to spend so great that to satisfy it they have to borrow money and go into debt? Let's see how frugal we are today and compare this with families in 1980.

U.S. Consumer Debt, 1980 and 2003			
Year	**Total Debt**	**Total Debt per Person Current $**	**Total Debt per Person Constant $ (2003)**
1980	$302 billion	$1,336	$2,983
2003	$2,025 billion	$6,958	$6,958

(continued)

DBQ 19: HOW HAS AMERICAN SOCIETY CHANGED SINCE 1980? *CONTINUED*

Average U.S Personal Savings Rates, 1980–2005	
Average Rate for 1980s	9%
Average Rate for 1990s	5.2%
Average Rate for 2000–2005	1.9%

How frugal are Americans today compared with Americans twenty-five years ago?

_____

Are today's personal spending, borrowing, and saving practices good or bad for the future of our country? Explain. _____

_____

Document 7

Many workers earn only the federal minimum hourly wage. Let's see how this wage has changed from 1980 to the present.

U.S. Federal Minimum Wage—Hourly Pay Rate						
	1980	1985	1990	1995	2000	2005
Current Dollars	$3.10	$3.35	$3.80	$4.25	$5.15	$5.15
Constant Dollars (1980)	$3.10	$4.04	$4.92	$5.73	$6.48	$7.35*

* If the minimum wage had increased at the rate of inflation from 1980 to 2005, it would have risen to $7.35. This means that 2005's hourly minimum wage of $5.15 was really $2.20 lower than it was in 1980.

What does today's lower minimum wage rate mean for low-wage workers? _____

_____

_____

PART B Essay: In what important ways has American society changed since 1980?

DBQ 20: YOUR FUTURE: WHAT WILL IT BE LIKE?

You know some of the ways that American life has changed in the years since 1980. Those were the years when your parents grew from their teens into adulthood and then into middle age. For most of your parents, these years included their graduation from high school, the launching of careers, marriage, and children. Many graduated from college, or served in the armed forces, and purchased homes. Some relocated, moving far from where they had been born and raised. Many are happy with these years and what these decades brought to them. Others are disappointed.

It's easy to look back in history. It's much more difficult to look forward into the future. Predicting the future is like forecasting the weather. Short-term predictions are fairly accurate. But predictions that are far off are much less certain. Long-term predictions mean weeks or months for the weather forecaster. They mean decades or centuries for the social scientist.

Long-term forecasting is done by looking at trends and patterns. These trends are plotted from the past into the present. Then they are projected into the future. The best long-term forecasting takes into account recent changes or factors that are likely to affect the projection.

This DBQ asks you to forecast your future. It provides you some trend lines and patterns and asks you to project them into the future. It also provides some recent factors that will probably affect your lives.

■ **Directions:** The following question is based on the documents (1–5) that follow. Before reading these documents, be sure to

1. Carefully read and think about the document-based question that follows these directions.

2. Ask yourself: What do I already know about this question and its topic? What did I learn from reading the Historical Background section? If I had to answer the document-based question without reading any of the documents, what would I say?

3. Take a few minutes to jot down the major things you already know about this topic and question. What important names, dates, events, and major ideas do you already know?

4. Now read each document carefully. Ask yourself: How does this document help to answer the document-based question? Underline things of special importance and jot notes in the margins. If you're confused by or don't understand a document, go on to the next one. Later, if you have time, you can go back.

5. Develop a thesis statement that directly answers the document-based question. You'll want to state this thesis early in your essay.

(continued)

DBQ 20: YOUR FUTURE: WHAT WILL IT BE LIKE? CONTINUED

6. Briefly outline your entire essay. Make sure that what you say in it supports and proves your thesis statement. In your essay, plan how you'll use the information found in the documents and what you know already about this topic.

7. Carefully write your essay. As you include supportive information from documents, be sure to cite the sources of this information. This will add authority and credibility to what you're saying.

Question: What will your life be like twenty-five years from now?

 PART A

The following documents will help you answer the document-based question. Read each document carefully. Answer the question or questions that follow each document.

Document 1

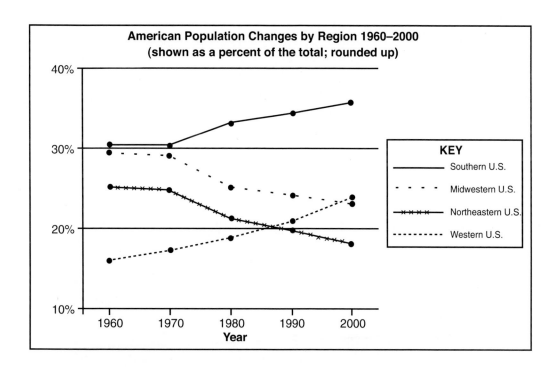

Which regions of our country are losing population? _____

Which are gaining population? _____

(continued)

DBQ 20: YOUR FUTURE: WHAT WILL IT BE LIKE? *CONTINUED*

Why do you suppose so many people are moving from some regions to others?

_____

_____

Document 2

Employment by Selected Economic Sectors, 1960–2003 (shown as a percent of total employment)			
	1960	**1980**	**2003**
Agriculture	4.5%	3.4%	2.4%
Mining	1.3%	1.1%	0.4%
Construction	5.4%	4.8%	6.0%
Manufacturing	31%	22%	14.8%
Transportation and public utilities	7.4%	5.7%	5%
Sales/trade	21%	23%	21%
Various services	14%	20%	26%
Government	15%	18%	26%

Which sectors of employment are in greatest decline? _____

Which employment sectors are growing?_____

Document 3

The following graphs show the urban, rural, and suburban population of the United States in 1950 and in 2000.

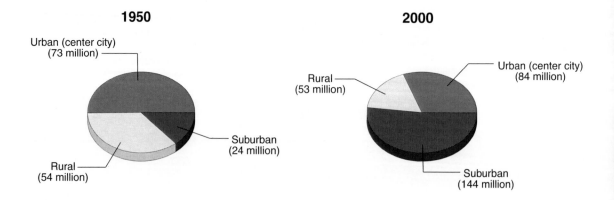

(continued)

DBQ 20: YOUR FUTURE: WHAT WILL IT BE LIKE? CONTINUED

Why do you suppose so many Americans moved into suburban communities over the past fifty years? _____

_____

Document 4

In 2005, the book *The World Is Flat: A Brief History of the Twenty-First Century* by journalist Thomas Friedman was published. It became a huge best-seller. The book told how the United States was entering into fierce economic competition with many other countries. The basis of this competition is technology. Those countries whose citizens are the best educated—and especially well educated in science, math, and engineering—will do well economically. Those who aren't will see declining standards of living in the twenty-first century.

One measure of the success of a nation's education in science, math, and technology is the International Test of Math and Science. This test is administered to students in many countries around the world. The most recent testing occurred in 2003. Here are some of the results from the math tests. U.S. students scored above the international average. But students from many other countries scored much higher.

Selected Math Scores—International Test of Math and Science, 2003			
Fourth-Grade Scores		**Eighth-Grade Scores**	
Singapore	610	Singapore	605
Hong Kong	575	South Korea	589
Japan	565	Hong Kong	586
China (Taipei)	564	China (Taipei)	585
Netherlands	540	Japan	570
Latvia	536	Belgium	537
Lithuania	534	Netherlands	536
Russia	532	Estonia	531
England	531	Hungary	529
Hungary	529	Malaysia	508
USA	518	Latvia	508
		Russia	508
Average Score	495	Slovak Rep.	508
		Australia	505
		USA	504
		Average Score	466

(continued)

129

Document-Based Assessment for U.S. History

DBQ 20: YOUR FUTURE: WHAT WILL IT BE LIKE?*CONTINUED*

What do these data say about our country's economic prospects in the twenty-first century? _____

_____

_____

Document 5

Our nation is facing a number of challenges in the near future. It's likely that they will affect you and your life. Here are four of those challenges.

Growth of the National Debt

Since 1980, the federal government has borrowed not just millions, or billions, but trillions of dollars. Look at this chart.

U.S. National Debt		
	Total Debt	**Per Capita Debt (debt per person)**
1980	$0.9 trillion	$4,000
1990	$3.6 trillion	$14,500
2000	$5.7 trillion	$20,180
2005	$8.0 trillion	$26,700

How will this debt be paid off? _____

_____

Who will pay for it? _____

_____

Aging of the Population

An aging population will present the United States with huge medical bills and pension costs. The costs of Social Security will skyrocket. (Social Security is the national retirement supplement program. It is supported by taxes on all Americans.)

(continued)

DBQ 20: YOUR FUTURE: WHAT WILL IT BE LIKE? *CONTINUED*

U.S. Population Age 65 and Older		
Year	Number of Americans Age 65 and Older	% of the Total U.S. Population Age 65 and Older
1900	3 million	4.1%
1950	12 million	8.1%
1970	20 million	9.8%
1980	26 million	11.3%
1990	31 million	12.5%
2000	35 million	12.4%
2010*	40 million	13.0%
2020*	55 million	16.3%
2030*	71 million	19.6%
*Estimates		

How will the aging of America affect you during your life? _____

_____

_____

The Pension Crisis

Pensions are income plans designed to support retired workers in their older years. Your grandparents lived and worked at a time when businesses commonly provided pensions. Some of your parents still have company pension plans. Typically, company pension plans require that workers and the company contribute payments each month through the years of the workers' employment. If workers continue with the company for a long time, these contributions will add up to a sizable sum. The workers can then retire and draw on this fund for income during their older years.

In recent years the number of businesses providing workers with company pensions has dropped. In 1960 over 40 percent of nongovernment workers had company pensions. Today, fewer than 20 percent do. Corporations facing economic hard times have dropped their pensions. These include huge companies like Bethlehem Steel, Pan American Airlines, and Kaiser Aluminum. Millions of workers have found themselves with severely reduced pensions or with no money at all as they face old age.

(continued)

DBQ 20: YOUR FUTURE: WHAT WILL IT BE LIKE? CONTINUED

Here is a chart showing how the number of company-provided pension plans has declined over the past several decades.

Number of Private-Sector Pension Plans, 1980–2004

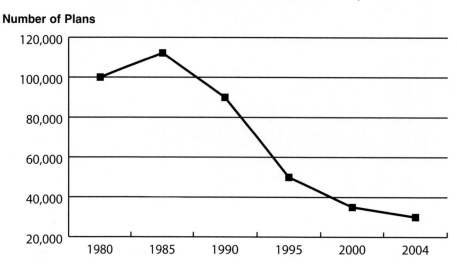

How will the pension crisis affect your life? _____

_____

_____

The Rising Costs of Health Care

Medical costs, 1960–2000				
	Total $	**Percent of GNP**	**$ per Household**	**$ per Capita**
1960	$ 27 billion	5.3%	$ 510	$ 151
1970	$ 74 billion	7.4%	$ 1,170	$ 365
1980	$250 billion	9.2%	$ 3,090	$1,101
1990	$675 billion	12.2%	$ 7,250	$2,711
2000	$1,400 billion	15.4%	$13,000	$5,000

What challenges to your adult life do you see in this chart? _____

_____

_____

PART B

Essay: What will your life be like twenty-five years from now?

Grading Key

DBQ 1: WHAT MOTIVATED EUROPEANS TO EXPLORE AMERICA?

Document 1
One of the purposes of early European exploration of the Americas was to bring Christianity to the "residents and inhabitants." Columbus and other early European explorers accepted and followed this directive by the pope.

Document 2
Columbus and his financial supporters, including the Spanish king and queen, hoped that gold, silver, and other products of great value would be discovered. This desire for wealth was clearly a motive of exploration. (Of course, the economic motive—the desire to trade with Asia—was Europe's primary objective.)

Document 3
Columbus and most of the other early explorers weren't hoping to find a New World. They were trying to find a water route to Asia. When it finally became obvious that America was a large "obstacle" in their way, explorers worked to find a passageway around or through America. This search for the fabled Northwest Passage to Asia became a major motive of exploration of America for many years following Columbus's first voyage.

ADDITIONAL INFORMATION BEYOND THE DOCUMENTS
The documents provide students with only fragments of information and evidence. Students' answers should include relevant information learned in classroom lessons, from the textbook, and from other sources beyond just these few documents. The following list suggests some of the concepts, people, and events that students could include from this outside learning.

Maya, Aztec, and Inca cultures
Prince Henry of Portugal
conquistadores
Renaissance
Treaty of Tordesillas
New Spain
Reformation
Cortez and Coronado
African slave trade
Age of Exploration
Spanish missions
Ponce de León
Vikings
Northwest Passage

DBQ 2: WHY AND HOW DID PEOPLE COME TO EARLY AMERICA?

Document 1
Many slaves were brought to America after being kidnapped and sold in Africa. These people were "involuntary" immigrants.

Document 2
Many early American colonists came as indentured servants. Most of them were poor people who voluntarily came to America, choosing to pay the cost of passage through "selling" their labor for several years. Some indentured servants came to the colonies involuntarily as transported convicts from England.

Document 3
Many poor tenant farmers were attracted to the colonies by the promise of free land. No doubt many indentured themselves to pay the cost of transport to America.

Document 4
Some Europeans, such as the New England Puritans, came to the American colonies for religious freedom.

Document 5
Many European immigrants came to the American colonies to escape social injustices and oppression and in search of greater opportunities and better lives.

ADDITIONAL INFORMATION BEYOND THE DOCUMENTS
The documents provide students with only fragments of information and evidence. Students' answers should include relevant information learned in classroom lessons, from the textbook, and from other sources beyond just these few documents. The following list suggests some of the concepts, people, and events that students could include from this outside learning.

Georgia's James Oglethorpe
Protestant Reformation
headrights
New Netherlands
plantations
Quakers
Lord Baltimore and Maryland's Catholic haven
the enclosure movement
triangular trade
fur trade, lumber, shipbuilding, and tobacco
mercantilism
Pennsylvania "Dutch"

DBQ 3: WHAT CAUSED THE AMERICAN REVOLUTION?

Document 1
Adams condemned the Stamp Act because it was imposed on American colonists by a legislature (the British Parliament) that had no representatives elected by the colonists. Thus, the Stamp Act was "taxation without representation." Adams also criticized the method of enforcing the Stamp Act, which allowed trials without juries.

Document 2

Colonists were angered by, and fearful of, the Declaratory Act's claim of total power over them. It was, to them, a threat of tyranny.

Document 3

Just as the Stamp Act had been, the Townshend Acts were "taxation without representation." Perceptive students may comment on the hyperbole in Dickinson's prose—a characteristic of propaganda and political promotion.

Document 4

Many students will comment on the obvious bias of Revere's depiction of the Boston Massacre. Clearly, it was designed to promote an anti-British feeling.

Document 5

The resolutions of the 1774 First Continental Congress listed a number of British actions that violated the rights and liberties of the American colonists. Foremost among them were "several acts" that unlawfully imposed taxes on the colonists. Various other violations of the colonists' rights followed as the British attempted to enforce the unlawful taxes.

ADDITIONAL INFORMATION BEYOND THE DOCUMENTS

The documents provide students with only fragments of information and evidence. Students' answers should include relevant information learned in classroom lessons, from the textbook, and from other sources beyond just these few documents. The following list suggests some of the concepts, people, and events that students could include from this outside learning.

> Proclamation of 1763
> mercantilism
> Virginia House of Burgesses
> King George III
> John Hancock
> Quebec Act
> Sugar Act
> George Grenville
> The Association
> Sam Adams
> colonial boycotts
> Patrick Henry
> direct and indirect taxation

DBQ 4: THE NEW CONSTITUTION: SHOULD IT BE APPROVED?

Document 1

Amos Singletary opposed the Constitution. He expressed the feelings of many farmers and people of modest means. Remembering the abuses of the British Parliament, they feared creating a new, powerful central government. They also worried that this new government would be controlled by the rich and powerful ("men of learning, and moneyed men") and then "swallow up all us little folks."

Document 2

Mercy Otis Warren also opposed the Constitution, fearing the erection of a powerful central government that would endanger the rights and freedoms of the people and threaten the authority and independence of the states. She objected to the omission of a Bill of Rights that could protect these rights and freedoms.

Document 3

This newspaper editorial spoke in favor of the Constitution. Its author hoped that a "new, a protecting, and efficient federal government" would be able to solve the economic problems and protect the United States from foreign insults. One would guess that Shays' Rebellion and the state governments' ineffective response to it had frightened this author.

Document 4

Barlow supported the new Constitution, fearing that "without an efficient [national] government," America's independence would "cease to be a blessing." He also believed that creating a strong national government would complete the Revolution.

Document 5

Jay favored the Constitution. He began by reminding his readers that the Constitution "comes recommended to you" by respected American leaders, and he asked that the public "give the proposed Constitution a fair trial." It could, he pointed out, be improved (amended) as needed in the future.

Document 6

Jefferson had reservations about the Constitution. Like Warren (in Document 2), he feared that a powerful national government would threaten the freedoms of the people. A bill of rights should be added. It's "what the people are entitled to," Jefferson declared.

ADDITIONAL INFORMATION BEYOND THE DOCUMENTS

The documents provide students with only fragments of information and evidence. Students' answers should include relevant information learned in classroom lessons, from the textbook, and from other sources beyond just these few documents. The following list suggests some of the concepts, people, and events that students could include from this outside learning.

> Articles of Confederation
> constitutional compromises
> checks and balances
> interstate commerce issues
> foreign trade problems
> Patrick Henry
> *Federalist Papers*
> Federalists and Anti-Federalists
> separation of powers
> Alexander Hamilton
> Northwest Ordinance
> Bill of Rights
> Benjamin Franklin
> state-issued paper currency

DBQ 5: WHAT CHALLENGES DID GEORGE WASHINGTON FACE AS PRESIDENT?

Document 1
The resolution suggests that Virginia opposed Hamilton's plan to pay the debts of the states because the legislature believed that the Constitution gave no such power to the federal government. But we might assume that Virginia was one of those states that had little or no state debt and resented having to pay the debts of less fiscally sound states.

Document 2
Jefferson opposed Hamilton's plan to establish a national bank, believing it beyond the power granted to the federal government by the Constitution. Additionally, he felt that the national bank was an illegal monopoly and that Hamilton's plan for it violated the authority of the states.

Document 3
Clearly, Jefferson believed Hamilton was a danger to the nation. Jefferson claimed that Hamilton supported monarchy and corruption and that he was a thoughtless supporter of Great Britain. In turn, Hamilton believed Jefferson was a danger to the nation, especially as Jefferson, Madison, and their followers opposed Hamilton's plans.

Document 4
Washington feared that the United States might be drawn into the war on one side or the other (especially since Jefferson and Hamilton were already taking sides). Knowing that we were still a young and weak nation, Washington wanted to keep the United States isolated from Europe's wars.

Document 5
Washington saw the Whiskey Rebellion as a challenge to the authority of the new federal government. To let it succeed would undermine public support for the government. No doubt Hamilton strongly supported this resolution, Jefferson less so.

Document 6
In his Farewell Address, Washington spoke out on two issues that had troubled his entire presidency — the threat of being drawn into the European war (because of our Revolutionary War alliance with France) and the danger of U.S. national unity being endangered by warring political factions.

ADDITIONAL INFORMATION BEYOND THE DOCUMENTS
The documents provide students with only fragments of information and evidence. Students' answers should include relevant information learned in classroom lessons, from the textbook, and from other sources beyond just these few documents. The following list suggests some of the concepts, people, and events that students could include from this outside learning.

Jefferson vs. Hamilton
French Revolution
funding the national debt
constitutionalism
British impressment
national bank
urban vs. rural
Jay's Treaty
tariff
democracy
cabinet system
Indian wars in Ohio
agriculture vs. commerce
Bill of Rights

DBQ 6: WHY DO WE REMEMBER THOMAS JEFFERSON?

Document 1
Jefferson believed that all people possess certain basic rights including "Life, Liberty and the pursuit of Happiness." The primary purpose of government is to protect these rights. These are basic tenets of political liberalism.

Document 2
Essential principles of liberal government are the right of election by the people, and basic civil liberties such as freedom of press and religion, and trial by jury. These are basic tenets of liberalism.

Document 3
Jefferson supported free public education for all. Public education would benefit not only individuals but also society as a whole, by creating a wise and sensible electorate. Such beliefs are basic to liberalism.

Document 4
Jefferson defended the rights of the minority against the potential oppression of the majority. This tolerance for, and protection of, minority viewpoints and interests is basic to liberalism.

Document 5
Jefferson generally supported a liberal immigration policy. He recognized the value of immigration and hoped that government would extend rights and opportunities to new immigrants.

ADDITIONAL INFORMATION BEYOND THE DOCUMENTS
The documents provide students with only fragments of information and evidence. Students' answers should include relevant information learned in classroom lessons, from the textbook, and from other sources beyond just these few documents. The following list suggests some of the concepts, people, and events that students could include from this outside learning.

Virginia Statute for Religious Freedom
University of Virginia
slavery
French Revolution
Democratic-Republican Party
Monticello
secretary of state

Document-Based Assessment for
U.S. History

Alien and Sedition Acts
Louisiana Purchase
conflicts with Hamilton
Virginia and Kentucky Resolutions

DBQ 7: INDIAN REMOVAL: IS IT JUSTIFIED?

Document 1
President Monroe argued that removal of the Cherokees and other southeastern tribes would "shield them from impending ruin," and "promote their welfare and happiness." No doubt, some students will question his sincerity.

Document 2
President Jackson supported Georgia, calling for Congress to set aside lands in the West, beyond the Mississippi, for the southeastern tribes. More than a few students will doubt Jackson's objectivity, pointing to his past as an Indian fighter. No doubt some students will scoff at the "guarantee" that these lands would belong to the Indians "as long as they shall occupy" them.

Document 3
The Cherokees pleaded with Congress to uphold their treaty rights and to protect them from Georgia's (and President Jackson's) attempt to force them off of their lands.

Document 4
The Indian Removal Act called for the setting aside of lands in the West, beyond the Mississippi, for the resettlement of the southeastern tribes. Again, some students will question the sincerity of many of the assurances to the Indians.

Document 5
Lewis Cass supported Georgia, arguing that the Cherokees should be relocated west of the Mississippi. According to Cass, the southeastern Indian tribes were "barbarous people . . . [who] cannot live in contact with a civilized community." It's likely that some students will question Cass's sincerity.

Document 6
Senator Frelinghuysen was pleading for the Cherokees and the other southeastern tribes. Time after time Americans had taken the Indians' lands, so that now they were "crowded . . . upon a few miserable acres." Still, in their greed, the Americans demanded more. Clearly, Frelinghuysen wanted to shame his colleagues into protecting the Indians and their lands.

ADDITIONAL INFORMATION BEYOND THE DOCUMENTS
The documents provide students with only fragments of information and evidence. Students' answers should include relevant information learned in classroom lessons, from the textbook, and from other sources beyond just these few documents.

Because students' essays are simulated newspaper editorials from the spring of 1830, they will find it impossible to cite much of what they've learned about this historical episode. Events after the spring of 1830 include the Trail of Tears, Chief

Justice Marshall's decision in the case of *Worcester* v. *Georgia*, the Seminoles' resistance under the leadership of Osceola, and other events that occurred as a result of the passage of the Indian Removal Act.

Postscript: Congress narrowly passed the Indian Removal Act of 1830 on May 26, and President Jackson signed it on May 28. In a formal message to Congress later that year, President Jackson proudly announced that soon, "a dense and civilized population [of Americans]" will settle "large tracts of country now occupied by a few savage hunters." During the following ten years, almost 100,000 Indians from the southeastern states were coerced into giving up their lands. Over those years, the Indians were marched west in dozens of groups under guard of military troops. Along the way, thousands died—so many, that the Indians came to call these "the Trails of Tears."

DBQ 8: HOW DID SLAVERY LEAD TO THE CIVIL WAR?

Document 1
Jefferson was frightened that the issue of slavery (raised by the Missouri crisis) was so divisive that it would eventually destroy the United States.

Document 2
Students should see that the election of 1860 broke the political alliance of the South and the West. Now the Republican Party had linked the West to the North. Southern defenders of slavery feared that, with the South now an isolated minority region, slavery was threatened because it would not be allowed to spread west.

Document 3
Senator Chase (and many other Northerners) strongly opposed the Kansas-Nebraska Act because it raised the possibility that slavery could spread to sections of the West that had been closed to slavery by the 1820 Missouri Compromise. Some students will note that this issue, more than any other, destroyed the national Whig Party and created the Northern Republican Party. Chase and other northern opponents of slavery became firm in their conviction that slavery had to be confined to those states where it presently existed. It could not be allowed to spread west.

Document 4
In the famous Lincoln-Douglas debates, Lincoln predicted that slavery would divide the nation. Impress upon students that this is an important speech in U.S. history—one of Lincoln's most famous.

Document 5
The Republican Party platform of 1860 was adamant—slavery would not be allowed to spread west into new states. Some students will note that, while Lincoln strongly supported this plank of the platform, he also assured the slaveholding states that he would not attack slavery where it presently existed.

Document 6

The South Carolina Declaration identified Lincoln's (and the Republican Party's) opposition to slavery as a justification for secession.

Document 7

In Lincoln's March 4 Inaugural Address, he identified the conflict between the North and South over the possible extension of slavery into the West as the "only substantial dispute."

ADDITIONAL INFORMATION BEYOND THE DOCUMENTS

The documents provide students with only fragments of information and evidence. Students' answers should include relevant information learned in classroom lessons, from the textbook, and from other sources beyond just these few documents. The following list suggests some of the concepts, people, and events that students could include from this outside learning.

> nullification
> Mexican War
> William Lloyd Garrison
> tariff crisis
> Wilmot Proviso
> popular sovereignty
> states' rights
> Bleeding Kansas
> Fugitive Slave Law
> abolitionists
> John Brown
> John C. Calhoun
> Nat Turner
> Harpers Ferry
> Free Soil Party
> Underground Railroad
> Frederick Douglass
> Crittenden Compromise
> Dred Scott case

DBQ 9: WHY DID THE SOUTH LOSE THE CIVIL WAR?

Document 1

The North clearly had industrial superiority, and this greatly helped its war effort in many ways—in the production of guns and artillery and uniforms and supplies, in the rapid movement of men and supplies, and so on.

Document 2

The North, with its much larger population, had a greater ability to provide soldiers, and to keep the farms and factories operating on the home front. While the existence of 3.5 million slaves in the South helped to ensure that farms and plantations continued to operate, it also required that significant numbers of white men remain at home to supervise and guard the slave population. These men could not, then, serve in the armies, adding to the shortage of southern soldiers.

Document 3

As some historians would say, "King Cotton was dethroned by Kings Wheat and Corn." Because new sources of cotton were found in Egypt and India and because of increased importation of food products from the North, European public opinion turned increasingly to support the North.

Document 4

Most Europeans opposed slavery. Once Lincoln's Emancipation Proclamation made the abolition of slavery an avowed purpose of the Union, public opinion in France and England turned against the South.

Document 5

This will not be an easy concept for students to understand. Teachers may find it helpful to compare the political weakness of the Confederate States with the problems faced in earlier times under the Articles of Confederation. Political unity is necessary for a strong national military effort.

ADDITIONAL INFORMATION BEYOND THE DOCUMENTS

The documents provide students with only fragments of information and evidence. Students' answers should include relevant information learned in classroom lessons, from the textbook, and from other sources beyond just these few documents. The following list suggests some of the concepts, people, and events that students could include from this outside learning.

> Ulysses S. Grant
> African-American soldiers
> Pickett's charge
> Battle of Gettysburg
> blockade runners
> Radical Republicans
> Battle of Vicksburg
> Battle of Antietam
> Copperheads
> William T. Sherman
> Lincoln vs. Davis
> Appomattox
> Thirteenth Amendment
> draft riots

DBQ 10: RECONSTRUCTION: A NOBLE EFFORT, OR OPPRESSION AND PUNISHMENT?

Teachers should point out to students that the debate over voting rights for southern ex-slaves revolved only around the question of black men voting. Voting rights for black women were not on the table, any more than voting rights for white women were at this time in any politically feasible way.

Document 1

The Convention of Colored Men pleaded with Congress to empower the southern freedmen with the right to vote.

It would be their only protection against the southern whites. Additionally, it would help to "defend . . . Federal Liberty from the treason" of the former Confederates.

Document 2
The Virginia Colored Citizens Convention also pleaded with Congress. The right to vote would provide protection to the freed southern ex-slaves. "Give us this, and we will protect ourselves."

Document 3
Stevens is candid in this statement. His support for voting rights for the southern freedmen grew from several motives: It was just and right; it would protect them and their Southern white allies; it would continue Republican political control of the nation. Some students will also cite Stevens's comment from the Historical Background section.

Document 4
President Johnson believed that the congressional Republicans wanted to enfranchise the freed slaves solely for the crass political purpose of keeping the Republican Party in power.

Document 5
Dunning believed most northern Republicans were hypocrites and insincere in their advocacy of voting rights for the southern blacks. Many of these politicians came from northern states where black citizens were denied the right to vote. Clearly, the Republican congressional leaders supported black voting in the South solely to keep the Republican Party in power.

Document 6
Stampp, while understanding the mixed motives of congressional Republicans for supporting the franchise for the southern ex-slaves, nonetheless saw great honesty, sincerity, and idealism in the purposes of many of the northern Republican congressmen. Many had been abolitionists and advocates of racial justice for years. Their support for civil rights for the southern blacks after the Civil War was only a continuation of their earlier idealism.

ADDITIONAL INFORMATION BEYOND THE DOCUMENTS
The documents provide students with only fragments of information and evidence. Students' answers should include relevant information learned in classroom lessons, from the textbook, and from other sources beyond just these few documents. The following list suggests some of the concepts, people, and events that students could include from this outside learning.

> Wade-Davis Bill
> Fifteenth Amendment
> segregation
> Ten-Percent Plan
> Scalawags
> Jim Crow
> Fourteenth Amendment
> Carpetbaggers
> Ku Klux Klan
> impeachment of Johnson

sharecroppers
Democratic "redemption"
election of 1876

DBQ 11: HOW DID THE UNITED STATES CHANGE IN THE DECADES AFTER THE CIVIL WAR?

Document 1
America's population increased by almost 2 1/2 times during this forty-year period. Almost the entire western region of the nation became settled. (Be sure that students understand that most western plains and mountain states were agricultural. Their settlement density was—and is—much less than many other states.)

Document 2
Industrialism flourished during this time, but so too did agriculture—especially western wheat and corn. The workforce increasingly worked in nonfarm employment.

Document 3
In 1860, only eight cities had populations greater than 100,000. Forty years later, in 1900, over thirty cities had populations larger than 100,000. Clearly, the United States was rapidly becoming a nation of cities and factories.

Document 4
During the decades following the Civil War, the South declined greatly in wealth, while the Northeast and industrial Midwest rose to economic dominance. Why? The destruction of the Civil War was a cause; so too was the South's continued dependence on agriculture. No doubt the sharecropping system also contributed to economic stagnation in this region. But industrialization in the Northeast and Midwest probably was the major reason for the comparative changes in regional wealth.

Document 5
Increasing numbers of immigrants were coming to the United States to work in factories and mines. Many also came to take up homesteads in the northern Great Plains and prairie states.

ADDITIONAL INFORMATION BEYOND THE DOCUMENTS
The documents provide students with only fragments of information and evidence. Students' answers should include relevant information learned in classroom lessons, from the textbook, and from other sources beyond just these few documents. The following list suggests some of the concepts, people, and events that students could include from this outside learning.

> Reconstruction
> Andrew Carnegie
> monopolies
> sharecropping
> John Deere
> Jim Crow

Bessemer process
new immigrants
Cornelius Vanderbilt
electricity
Ellis Island
George Pullman
tariffs
Homestead Act

DBQ 12: SHOULD FURTHER IMMIGRATION TO THE UNITED STATES BE RESTRICTED?

Document 1
American immigration changed greatly in the late nineteenth century. Its pace and magnitude increased by a large amount. Also, countries like Russia, Italy, and Poland, which earlier sent almost no immigrants, became major sources of immigrants.

Document 2
According to Strong, many immigrants became criminals. Strong also worried that the process of assimilation was becoming more difficult as the number of immigrants increased.

Document 3
The 1892 congressional report harshly condemned Chinese immigrants, arguing that their presence was a danger to the United States and its values.

Document 4
This labor union leader chided those who opposed immigration, pointing out that in earlier times they, or their ancestors, had been subjects of similar anti-immigration sentiment.

Document 5
Senator Lodge argued that unrestricted immigration forced down wage rates and thus threatened the American standard of living. But a greater fear was that immigration threatened "the quality of our citizenship." Whereas, in earlier times, immigrants were "kindred people" to Americans, Lodge claimed that more recent immigrants were a "lower race" who threatened not only U.S. decline but also the decline of "human civilization."

Document 6
This shows that much of the nativist movement of the late nineteenth century was virulently anti-Catholic.

Document 7
President Cleveland felt that unrestricted immigration had greatly benefited the United States through all of its history. To now limit it, based on a person's educational opportunity, was wrong.

ADDITIONAL INFORMATION BEYOND THE DOCUMENTS
The documents provide students with only fragments of information and evidence. Students' answers should include relevant information learned in classroom lessons, from the textbook, and from other sources beyond just these few documents. The following list suggests some of the concepts, people, and events that students could include from this outside learning.

Know-Nothing party
"new immigration"
"old immigration"
Tweed Ring
Andrew Carnegie
settlement houses
Haymarket Square riot
Samuel Gompers
anti-Semitism
Pullman strike
urban machine politics
Ellis Island
1890s depression
melting pot
Jacob Riis

DBQ 13: HOW DID THE PROGRESSIVES ATTACK CHILD LABOR?

Document 1
The charts show that the children of the working class were physically smaller than and apparently not as healthy as the children of the middle class. This suggested that poverty and child labor stunted the growth and development of children.

Document 2
The chart suggests that child labor bred crime. Child labor "occupations" led to juvenile delinquency.

Document 3
Author Helen Campbell was trying to shock her readers with this story about the "little mothers." No doubt the readers were struck by the danger of this practice—both to the "little mothers" and to the infants in their care.

Document 4
The written description was meant to upset middle-class readers. No doubt Spargo also meant to shock these readers with the suggestion that such brutal child labor was an obstacle to children's religious development.

Document 5
This was designed to strike fear in Spargo's readers. Child labor was undermining the moral development of children. By allowing so many children to labor at adult jobs, American society was creating "arrogant, wayward, and defiant" future adults—and contributing to a lawless future.

Document 6
Here, Spargo says that child labor was ruining the health and vitality of children, making them unfit for successful adult life, preparing them for poverty and social dependency.

ADDITIONAL INFORMATION BEYOND THE DOCUMENTS
The documents provide students with only fragments of information and evidence. Students' answers should include relevant information learned in classroom lessons, from the textbook, and from other sources beyond just these few documents. The following list suggests some of the concepts, people, and events that students could include from this outside learning.

    Jacob Riis
    Upton Sinclair
    immigration
    Theodore Roosevelt
    Social Gospel movement
    socialism
    Florence Kelley
    Social Darwinism
    sweatshops
    Hull House
    compulsory education laws
    labor unions
    Triangle Shirtwaist factory fire

DBQ 14: THE GREAT WAR IN EUROPE: WERE WE RIGHT TO FIGHT?

Document 1
President Wilson believed that Germany's use of unrestricted submarine warfare was "in fact nothing less than war against . . . the United States."

Document 2
Senator Norris believed that the United States had not, in fact, acted neutrally as it had promised. He said that moneyed interests—banks and investors—would profit from U.S. entrance into the war, at the cost of "human suffering" and "untold danger."

Document 3
Senator La Follette claimed that "9 out of 10" communications he had received from Americans opposed U.S. involvement in the war. But, he added, the voices of the poor were not being heard in this debate, even though the poor were the ones who would end up fighting the war.

Document 4
Most Americans remembered our nation's participation in World War I as a mistake.

Document 5
Each of these actions had added to Americans' animosity toward and fear of Germany. Germany's actions turned U.S. public opinion increasingly in support of England and France.

Document 6
The likelihood that American involvement had saved France and England from defeat by Germany will probably be cited by many students to support the position that American intervention in April 1917 was a correct decision.

ADDITIONAL INFORMATION BEYOND THE DOCUMENTS
The documents provide students with only fragments of information and evidence. Students' answers should include relevant information learned in classroom lessons, from the textbook, and from other sources beyond just these few documents. The following list suggests some of the concepts, people, and events that students could include from this outside learning.

    entangling alliances
    U-boats
    Henry Cabot Lodge
    nationalism
    Zimmerman Telegram
    Theodore Roosevelt
    Russian Revolution
    Fourteen Points
    Committee on Public Information
    Jeannette Rankin
    Espionage and Sedition Acts
    Red Scare
    Central Powers
    Treaty of Versailles
    war propaganda
    Allies
    League of Nations

DBQ 15: WHAT CAUSED THE GREAT DEPRESSION?

Document 1
Consumer spending after the stock market crash severely dropped. This drop in consumer demand then fed the cycle of overproduction . . . workers being laid off . . . further drop in consumer spending, and so on.

Document 2
American farmers had increased production during the war in response to Europe's greater demand for farm products. Once the war ended and exports to Europe dropped, American farmers faced a glut of farm produce and a consequent drop in farm prices. With their incomes severely reduced, farm families cut back on their purchases of consumer products, reducing consumer demand throughout the economy.

Document 3
Once families found themselves too deeply in debt, they severely cut back on their purchases of consumer goods. This contributed to U.S. economic overproduction and under-consumption.

Document 4
Help students understand how a broader distribution of wealth results in greater consumer demand. In the hands of one wealthy family, one million dollars will result in little spending. Instead, this money will be used for savings and investment. But one million dollars distributed to fifty middle-class families will largely be spent on consumer products.

ADDITIONAL INFORMATION BEYOND THE DOCUMENTS

The documents provide students with only fragments of information and evidence. Students' answers should include relevant information learned in classroom lessons, from the textbook, and from other sources beyond just these few documents. The following list suggests some of the concepts, people, and events that students could include from this outside learning.

speculation
"sick" industries
Black Tuesday
buying on margin
war debts
Dust Bowl
Mellon tax policies
unemployment compensation
labor unions
Herbert Hoover
high tariffs

DBQ 16: THE ELECTION OF 1936: SHOULD THE NEW DEAL CONTINUE?

Document 1

The Republicans charged that FDR and his New Deal were violating the Constitution by usurping the power of Congress, of the states, and of the people. The United States, they charged, was "in peril."

Document 2

The Republicans charged that FDR and his New Deal were wasting the taxpayers' money in extravagant programs that piled up deficits and threatened "national bankruptcy."

Document 3

The charts and graphs suggest that FDR's New Deal was moderately successful at solving the problems of the Great Depression. By 1936, unemployment had fallen from a high of 13.1 million in 1933 to 9.3 million, and the GNP had risen from $55.6 billion in 1933 to $82.5 billion. On the other hand, federal government borrowing (the deficit) had risen from $0 in 1930 to $4.4 billion in 1936. (Some perceptive students may point out that the large deficits began under Hoover.)

Document 4

Former president Hoover accused Roosevelt and his administration of subverting America's free institutions and personal liberties. However, the Republicans aimed to strengthen free institutions and personal liberties, Hoover said.

ADDITIONAL INFORMATION BEYOND THE DOCUMENTS

The documents provide students with only fragments of information and evidence. Students' answers should include relevant information learned in classroom lessons, from the textbook, and from other sources beyond just these few documents. The following list suggests some of the concepts, people, and events that students could include from this outside learning.

It's likely that most classroom instruction presents a relatively positive viewpoint of FDR and the New Deal. Yet most of the documents presented here provide a negative or ambivalent viewpoint of FDR. Consequently, teachers should expect that students will bring in lots of information from their classroom learning and not accept these few documents as representative, objective, and balanced viewpoints.

banking crisis
Social Security
The Grapes of Wrath
Bonus Army
Tennessee Valley Authority
Works Progress Administration
work relief agencies
direct relief
fireside chats
Frances Perkins
Agricultural Adjustment Act
Eleanor Roosevelt
Civilian Conservation Corps
Supreme Court actions

DBQ 17: WHAT WERE THE COSTS AND BENEFITS OF U.S. VICTORY IN WORLD WAR II?

Document 1

U.S. national defense expenditures rose from $1.1 billion in 1938 to $85.6 billion in 1945. Clearly, the economic costs of the war were immense.

Document 2

Because the United States was almost completely untouched directly by the war (other than Japan's December 7, 1941, attack on Pearl Harbor and some later fighting in Alaska's Aleutian Islands), the United States suffered very few civilian casualties. Other countries in which major fighting occurred suffered horrendous civilian casualties.

Document 3

The United States was economically supreme in 1945, and because it took other countries decades to rebuild their economies, the U.S. economic head start lasted for over a generation. But, as Friedman says, this gave Americans a "huge sense of entitlement and complacency," making us largely unprepared for the onslaught of global economic competition in our own times.

Document 4

Most Americans expected, with the U.S. victory in 1945, to be able to return to their quiet, isolated, and secure lives. But instead of this, Americans found themselves facing a new threat and greater insecurity.

Document 5

Most students will see the U.S. sole possession of the atomic bomb in 1945 as a benefit and opportunity. (Clearly, in 1945, most Americans would have agreed.) But a few especially thoughtful students will question this smug assumption.

Document-Based Assessment for
U.S. History

ADDITIONAL INFORMATION BEYOND THE DOCUMENTS

The documents provide students with only fragments of information and evidence. Students' answers should include relevant information learned in classroom lessons, from the textbook, and from other sources beyond just these few documents. The following list suggests some of the concepts, people, and events that students could include from this outside learning.

> United Nations
> Franklin Roosevelt
> Manhattan Project
> Berlin
> Truman Doctrine
> Winston Churchill
> "iron curtain" speech
> Harry Truman
> NATO
> Joseph Stalin
> Yalta Conference
> Marshall Plan
> A-bomb and H-bomb
> containment policy

DBQ 18: HOW DID THE UNITED STATES CHANGE IN THE POSTWAR YEARS?

Document 1

In the years following the war, the marriage and birthrates jumped. Indeed, in the mid-1950s the U.S. birthrate was almost twice what it is today.

Document 2

Consumer prosperity marked the postwar decades. In the fifteen years between 1935 and 1950, the number of cars on the road almost doubled, and the number of radios in American homes quadrupled. By 1950, there were eight million televisions in American homes. Americans in the postwar years became much more mobile, and they began to spend lots of time watching television.

Document 3

Growth in rural areas of the United States remained stagnant, cities grew by about 15 percent, and suburbs grew by over 200 percent! The American middle class moved to suburbia.

Document 4

Prewar America was marked by the Great Depression. Postwar America was marked by widespread prosperity. Indeed, between 1935 and 1945, per capita (real) income almost doubled. Also, according to this chart, this postwar prosperity continued through the 1950s.

Document 5

The move from farm to factory, from rural America to urban America, continued through the postwar decades. Document 5 reinforces the message of Document 3.

Document 6

As the men went overseas, American women moved into the labor market. By 1944, 42 percent of adult women held jobs outside of the home. But when the men came home, many women gave up their jobs. This document, together with Document 1, suggests that in the immediate postwar years many women got married, had children, and stayed home with those children. Clearly, this trend was reversed in the following years; today most women hold jobs outside the home.

ADDITIONAL INFORMATION BEYOND THE DOCUMENTS

The documents provide students with only fragments of information and evidence. Students' answers should include relevant information learned in classroom lessons, from the textbook, and from other sources beyond just these few documents. The following list suggests some of the concepts, people, and events that students could include from this outside learning.

> GI Bill
> Rosie the Riveter
> rock and roll
> mass advertising
> baby boom
> commuters
> Cold War
> popular culture
> Levittown
> Sunbelt migration
> McCarthyism
> interstate highways
> fast food
> Harry Truman

DBQ 19: HOW HAS AMERICAN SOCIETY CHANGED SINCE 1980?

Document 1

Real household incomes have increased only modestly since 1980. In constant dollars, the increase was $3,800, an increase of less than 10 percent. Between 2000 and 2003, the real household income actually dropped.

Document 2

Today a school principal would probably compose the letter on her or his own computer and print it. Using today's technology, it would take much less time than in this document's scenario.

Document 3

Most of these are communications or information-processing inventions that employ computer technology. Today's teenager can communicate and send information in ways only dreamed of in 1980.

Document 4

Fast foods are unusually high in calories. Additionally, today's children are less physically active than children were in earlier times. It's no wonder that they weigh so much more.

Document 5

Employment of high school students increased from 1980 to 2005, so that today the vast majority of high school students hold part-time jobs during the school year. Is this "good or bad" for teenagers? Probably most teenagers think it's good. But it probably means that students are studying less, learning less, and perhaps sacrificing their academic (and life) futures.

Document 6

Americans are clearly much less frugal today than they were in 1980. This cannot be good for their futures or for the future of our country.

Document 7

Students will be shocked by these data. Low-wage workers who are earning only the federal minimum wage have a much lower standard of living than similar workers had in 1980.

ADDITIONAL INFORMATION BEYOND THE DOCUMENTS

The documents provide students with only fragments of information and evidence. Students' answers should include relevant information learned in classroom lessons, from the textbook, and from other sources beyond just these few documents. The following list suggests some of the concepts, people, and events that students could include from this outside learning.

Ronald Reagan
Sunbelt migration
AIDS
George H. W. Bush
end of the Cold War
environmental crisis
Bill Clinton
September 11, 2001
Hispanic immigration
George W. Bush
rise of terrorism
health care crisis
decline of manufacturing
war in Iraq

DBQ 20: YOUR FUTURE: WHAT WILL IT BE LIKE?

Document 1

The West and South are growing in population, while the Northeast and Midwest are in decline. Many people are following economic opportunities; others (the growing number of retirees) are seeking warmer climates.

Document 2

Students will see that manufacturing jobs are in rapid decline, while employment opportunities in services and government are growing.

Document 3

Students should note the huge growth in suburban population and the continued decline in rural population over the past

half century. The causes of this growth may include more cars, better highways, residential segregation by race and socioeconomics, middle-class affluence, and so on.

Document 4

The ITMS test results do not look good for the United States. Unless schools increase math and technology skills of our students (the future workforce), the United States may see economic declines in the twenty-first century.

Document 5

Four challenges are presented here: 1) The mushrooming national debt will require future taxpayers (these students) to pay higher taxes (or will lead to government-authorized inflation). 2) The aging population will need care. Students may predict that they'll actually be caring for aged parents and grandparents, or caring for them through higher taxes. 3) Company pensions are disappearing. Students will note that most of them will not have traditional company (defined-benefit) pensions. Most will have to save for their own retirements. 4) The huge and rapidly rising costs of health care in the United States will inevitably result in a national crisis.

ADDITIONAL INFORMATION BEYOND THE DOCUMENTS

The documents provide students with only fragments of information and evidence. Students' answers should include relevant information learned in classroom lessons, from the textbook, and from other sources beyond just these few documents. The following list suggests some of the concepts, people, and events that students could include from this outside learning.

deficits
college education
pollution
taxation
Social Security
global warming
Sunbelt growth
Medicare
oil and gas prices
tariffs
world trade
world terrorism
Baby Boom generation
crime rates
low saving rates

Student Answers to DBQ 4: The New Constitution: Should It Be Approved?

Each of these two essays was written by a seventh grader in a sixty-minute class period. The students, led by the teacher, had read and discussed the question and closely reviewed the documents the day before in class. Minor writing mistakes are duplicated in the typed versions. Assessment comments and scores (using the rubric found on page *x-xi*) follow each essay.

Student Essay #1 (by Todd B.)

Today the states have a choice to ratify or not ratify the new Constitution. The Articles of Confederation are not going as well as planned because the states have to much power. The delegates in Philadelphia tried to revise the Articles, but ended up throwing them out and starting a new Constitution from scratch. The Federalists and Anti-federalists now are arguing over the new Constitution. They are trying to convince others to vote or not vote for the Constitution. If the people vote for the Constitution, I promise that we'll all have a better life.

I believe that we should ratify the Constitution. Under the new Constitution we'll have three branches of government instead of one. The Legislative branch under the new Constitution will be bicameral or have 2-houses. It's better than one branch of government because each branch will be able to check on the other to make sure nobody gets too much power.

I agree with the *Massachusetts Centinel* which talks about how people are poor and don't have jobs. Under the new Constitution we will have more job opportunities and we will earn more money. Since Shay's Rebellion states have continued to keep high taxes which people have had little money. Farmers fell into debt. People who could not pay the debts have had their property auctioned off. If they don't sell enough, they can be sent to jail. If we ratify the Constitution, then the states will lower their taxes and people can keep their money.

Joel Barlow is right. "The Revolution is but half complete. Independence and government were two objects [we fought] for, and but one is yet obtained." He means we've earned our independence, but not our government. If we don't get a strong central government, our independence will cease to exist.

The Constitution will change our lives for the better. The farmers can worry about farming, people can worry about jobs, while the government worries about the country. John Jay points out that the Constitution can be improved in the future. I agree with him. Even though the Articles could be improved, they weren't improved. It was unfair—9 out of 13 states had to approve. If the other 4 states didn't want that law, they had to deal with it anyway. The Constitution has a better chance of making fair changes because all 3 branches of government will vote on the changes. Thomas Jefferson points out to us that a Bill of Rights needs to be added. Even though I favor the ratification of the Constitution now, I agree with Jefferson.

We need a Bill of Rights to protect the people's rights.

Ever since the Articles of Confederation, things aren't going well. We now have a choice to ratify the Constitution or not ratify it. Now the Federalists and Anti-federalists are fighting more than ever to convince us to vote or not vote for the Constitution. If we ratify the Constitution things will be fair. For example, if you get in trouble in another state when the Constitution is ratified, they you might have a fair trial. Therefore, I think ratifying the Constitution is the best choice for our country.

This is a good answer, especially for a seventh grader. It stays true to the assigned question and format—being written as a newspaper editorial that supported or opposed the Constitution. It states a strong thesis—supporting ratification. While the student's understanding of the Constitution and the Articles is not very deep or sophisticated, for a seventh grader, it's pretty good. The same is true of his understanding of the times (the late 1780s) in context to the topic. His use of those documents that support his position is adequate, but he could do a better job of addressing (and countering) some of the opposing documents. On the other hand, he includes some pertinent and valuable information from his own knowledge of the topic. Finally, the essay is very well written—well organized, with forceful prose and mostly proper spelling, grammar, and mechanics. This essay was scored a weak 5.

Student Essay #2 (by Erica P.)

A new Constitution has just been made and the 13 states must decide to ratify it or not. Many people oppose the Constitution because it does not include a Bill of Rights. But on the other hand many people agree with the new Constitution because people think that we need a stronger national government so states won't get out of control. Everyone has their own oppinion about the Constitution, but in the end there will be a decision to ratify the Constitution or not.

I agree with the Constitution and I believe that the Constitution should be ratifyed. Many people oppose the Constitution because there is no Bill of Rights. In Document 5 it states "mend it as time, occasion, and experience may require." This means that the people can add a Bill of Rights to the Constitution when they feel it is necessary. Many respected men believe in ratifying the new Constitution including Benjamin Franklin, George Washington, James Madison, and John Jay. People should trust the knowledgeable judgment of these credible men. In document 1 people are afraid that the central government will become too powerful, but in fact, the states need a stronger central government because things won't be chaotic and other nations will respect the United States. The Constitution will accomplish this. Without a strong central government they can slack on paying taxes and then there is no money for the government. In document 3 the newspaper article is in favor of ratifying the Constitution. The states have created a bad image for themselves by fighting with each other. It is a sure sign that the Articles of Confederation are not working with little central government power. Document 4 states "Independence and government were the two objects [we fought] for, and but one is yet obtained." Americans still

ed to obtain their government. The only time the states have
d a real government was when the British controlled the
lonies. The only way to keep things from total chaos is to try
e new Constitution. The government will have controls so
en they won't get too powerful. For examples, separation of
wers and checks and balances. Separation of powers calls for
viding the government into 3 equil branches. Checks and
ances calls for each branch of government checking on the
hers. But checking on another branch they can check if that
anch is doing its job. If not, then that branch has the power to
 something about it. If people don't like a part of the
onstitution, it can be changed. Change may not always be
od, but in this case it will help the states tremendously.

e Constitution will help the states gane respect and more
portantly a government that can protect the people and have
ough power to run the 13 states. The only plan of
vernment that has not been tried will succede. I believe that

if people give the Constitution a chance they will grow to like
it. People must remember that this is a living Constitution.
People can change the Constitution when necessary. Our
government is in diar need of a stronger government.

While clearly not as good as the first essay, this still represents
a good job for a seventh grader. Though it loses some of its
focus (as a newspaper editorial), the essay states a clear
thesis—in support of the Constitution's ratification.
Additionally, the student understands the topic and question.
She uses most documents adequately, though showing a fairly
simplistic understanding of them. Additionally, she typically
commits a common student error—self-conscious citation of
documents, saying, as she did, "in document 5 it states . . . "
The essay includes some information from beyond the
documents (the discussion of checks and balances, for
example). Additionally, the essay is pretty well written. This
DBQ essay earned a score of 3+.